P9-DDB-368

CONTENTS

Acknowledgment

We are indebted to all those experts against whom we have played over the years and whom we have kibitzed. We especially thank those who have made lasting contributions to the current literature. A very special thanks goes to Larry Cohen for his advice, editing and encouragement. In addition, we owe a debt of gratitude to a cross-section of bridge players who took the time to review the book:

Bryan Coleman, Gene Fisher, Marty Graf, Julius Kozlove, Adrienne Kuehneman, Ann Lindley and Charlie Stenger.

FOREWORD

When Burt and Lynn first approached me with their "can't-miss" bridge book plans I had the expected skeptical reaction. "Mr. Cohen - - we've found a great way to show in writing how the experts play. We have a very unique way of explaining useful concepts..." I gave them my address and told them I'd take a look at a sample chapter if they wanted to mail it to me.

Several days later I received several chapters and I reluctantly read through them. I was prepared to send Burt and Lynn a polite notice of my disinterest as I've done with so many other manuscripts I've received from other "unknown" bridge writers who think they've unlocked the secrets of the universe.

This time was different. I was most pleasantly surprised by what I read. It was as if the authors had extracted a piece of my bridge brain and transcribed my way of thinking onto paper. Line after line, paragraph after paragraph they had clearly spelled out, well, "How the Experts Win at Bridge."

Not only did Burt and Lynn somehow capture the way the Rodwells and Zias think, but they divided it into well-organized chapters, charts and numerous examples that make the ideas exceedingly easy to digest. The way they explain the expert bidding philosophy in chapter two is a deadly accurate portrayal of the winning ways of *today's* national champions. It is indeed rare to find a bridge book which accurately describes how to safely dart in and out of auctions and create havoc for the opponents. Another real breakthrough-type highlight is the authors' "Five Lines of Defense" which is the simplest and most concise guide to defense that I've ever seen.

There are lots of instructional books on bridge, but this one truly delivers. The title is deadly accurate, and any astute reader should find their level of expertise improving dramatically. Be warned - - the ideas in these chapters are those of today's modern experts. This is not a description of 1950's conservative-style textbook bridge. The ideas put forth by the authors will not be condoned by the "establishment" of the bridge world. But how many events have they won lately?

Larry Cohen - Little Falls, NJ

INTRODUCTION

This book is for players, whether avid new ones, intermediate or advanced who would really like to improve their overall game. It is unique in two respects. First, the book outlines *the various concepts, principles and tactics used by experts at the table* --- how they win and how you can do the same. Secondly, the book deals with *the entire game of bridge*, something no other modern book has done.

Most books on bridge deal with individual aspects of the game. This book takes an integrated view of the *entire game*. The emphasis is not on endless rules but rather on how to think about the game. The book shows how experts handle *each aspect of the game* - bidding, declarer play, defense, opening leads and doubles in a matchpoint contest.

A special chapter then tells how experts modify these aspects of their game in major ways for team events and rubber bridge.

As we near the end of the book there are three chapters that are important building blocks for your overall bridge game. The first one describes how to build successful partnerships. The second helps you decide what your convention card should include. The third helps you devise your own self-study program to become the very best you can be.

How to Use This Book

Unlike much other bridge material, this is not a book you can just read through and drop. You will want to return to those areas where experience at the table shows a need to strengthen your game. Eventually, the concepts, principles and tactics involved will become second nature. For example, there are five lines of defense in bridge and you must be sufficiently acquainted with them to recognize the conditions that drive each one. With practice, the guidelines on defense will become instinctive and you will be on the road to success. In time the entire book will become a roadmap to winning bridge.

Chapter 1

WHERE THE MAJOR PAYOFFS ARE

Have you ever wondered which areas of your bridge game you might stress to significantly improve your results? If so, this book is for you. Below are the major payoff areas in bridge. They are highlighted through-out the book with (1) the best thinking of the experts in each area and (2) illustrations of how the payoffs are achieved.

The Major Payoffs

- *Getting your bid in early*

- *Disrupting the opponents' bidding*

- *Battling for partscores*

- *Judging the right time to push, defend or double*

- *Not straining for games and slams (MP)*

- *Emphasizing major suits and notrump (MP)*

- *Making extra tricks (MP)*

- *Taking sacrifices whenever feasible*

- *Choosing the right opening leads*

- *Being an unrelenting defender (MP)*

- *Doubling partscore contracts (MP)*

- *Taking advantage of favorable vulnerability*

- *Taking percentage actions*

- *Stressing frequency of success, not score size (MP)*

- *Playing "Partnership Bridge"*

- *Using proven modern conventions*

Figure 1-1

Most of the major payoff areas are equally applicable to any form of bridge - matchpoints, teams or rubber bridge. Several, however, are unique to matchpoints (see those earmarked MP) due to the method used to score pairs events.* The reasons are:

> **"Whether you win or lose the event depends on *how many* of your competitors you can outscore on each deal, by even the smallest of margins. This profoundly affects the strategy of the game, with every pair trying hard to get the most from each deal, in an effort to achieve that small but crucial edge."**
> **- Frank Stewart**

In the other forms of bridge - teams and rubber bridge - the environment is different and the approach to your game changes a lot. We'll cover all this in Chapter 7.

Regardless of the forms of bridge you like to play (many like them all), the important thing is to stress those actions that consistently pay off. This emphasis will increasingly make your game a winning one. Applying the principles involved in doing so is the subject of the remaining chapters of this book. To test whether you are truly picking up these important principles, you will find quizzes at the chapter's end.**

Good luck!

---

*For those who are interested, the appendix contains a further explanation of the scoring system for matchpoints and its implications.

**Most of the illustrations and quizzes used in this book are from well-known expert sources such as national championships, authoritative bridge books and magazines, the syndicated Sheinwold/Stewart newspaper column, and the Daily Bridge Calendar. The Calendar is published by Ashlar House, Inc./Copp Clark Ltd.; experts who contributed hands and analyses are Phillip Alder, Ted Horning, Eddie Kantar, Ron Klinger, Eric Kokish, Mike Lawrence and Bobby Wolff.

Chapter 2

HOW TOP EXPERTS BID

The basic strategy of experts is to always get their bids in early (the first shot). They operate on the premise that the first one to get information to their partner wins. When experts do **not** have the cards, their priority is maximum disruption. When the cards are fairly evenly **divided**, they bid aggressively at the lower levels for lead direction, partscores and saves. When experts **do** have the cards, they bid in a very disciplined manner.

Figure 2-1 highlights the bidding style and objectives of experts at the table. Notice how they vary depending on who's got the cards. Notice too that expert bidding objectives have one thing in common - - **getting your bid in early**.

Expert Bidding Style and Objectives

OBJECTIVES	STYLE
• **It's Not Their Hand** • Disrupt opponents • Direct leads • Sacrifice, if distributional	**Aggressive**
• **The Cards are Reasonably Divided** • Direct leads • Compete for partscores • Sacrifice if vulnerability permits • Balance in on fit auctions • Let opponents play misfits	**Aggressive**
• **It's Their Hand** • Bid only obvious games/slams • Double opponents when pushed (beyond "The Law") • Underbid flat hands, soft values, misfits • Favor notrump first, majors next, minors last	**Disciplined**

Figure 2-1

GET YOUR BID IN EARLY

It is well recognized today that matchpoints is a bidder's game. To get the process started, one person in the partnership has to get his bid in. Unless it is done early, the opportunity will usually disappear.

When you get your bid in early, all sorts of good things can happen. When you do not, there will be regrets; regrets that your partner missed the right opening lead, regrets that you did not push the opponents up one more level, regrets that you missed a partscore or even a game. On the other hand, the benefits of trap passing are all too rare to even consider as a strategy. The trap passer in top level competition today is practically extinct.

The only requirement for the initial bid is that it be as fully descriptive as possible of the distribution and high card values of the hand. Experts do not bid their hands piecemeal. For example, they do not overcall a suit if they have (1) notrump values or (2) a hand that can be better described with a two-suited bid. If you bid piecemeal in today's disruptive environment, you may never be able to reveal your full hand to your partner.

Preempt Whenever Practical

At the outset, experts often do not know whose hand it is. When it appears as though the opponents have the preponderance of the power, experts embark on a trouble-making style. Their purpose is to take space away from the opponents; to create havoc; and to interfere with or otherwise render the opponents' bidding machinery inoperative.

The modern trend is toward lighter and lighter preempts at all levels, unless the vulnerability is unfavorable. It is a marvelous way of getting your bid in - to ask for a lead, to compete for a partscore, to reach an otherwise difficult game, to prompt a sacrifice bid and, best of all, to disrupt the opponents. For example, what is your bid on this hand from the 1996 Spring North American Championships?

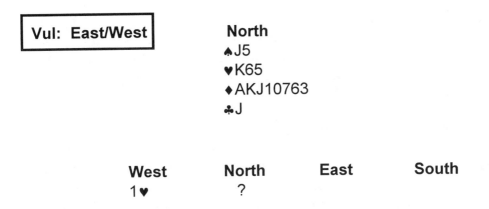

Vul: East/West

North
♠J5
♥K65
♦AKJ10763
♣J

West	North	East	South
1♥	?		

There are a number of options because of the *favorable vulnerability* but the most effective one that creates maximum disruption is 3NT. It literally blindsides the opponents and puts them to a maximum guess. The possibilities for your side are several. If the hand actually belongs to you, 3NT will probably make. If not, you may be allowed to play 3NT undoubled and fare better than if the opponents had played a partscore or game. If the opponents double, you can escape to 4D and still fare better if they have a game. In the actual case, the opponents had a 4H game but couldn't find it.

In the next case, you are playing against two national champions. They are vulnerable, you are not, and your partner opens 1H. Your right-hand opponent bids 2H, Michaels. What do you do?

Vul: East/West

South
♠42
♥J9743
♦K108542
♣ —

West	North	East	South
	1♥	2♥[1]	?

[1]Michaels

The actual South bid 5H. After two passes, the national champion doubled to show that his Michaels bid was a strong two-suiter (spades and a minor). His partner had a six-card club suit and no spade fit, so he passed the double, assuming his partner's minor was diamonds. North/South made 5H doubled and East/West missed their club slam. Note that when you take space away from the experts, they are reduced to guessing just like you.

The trend today is to preempt in all seats! The old-fashioned, more stringent requirements for preempting in first and second seat have pretty much disappeared. When you hold a preemptive hand the name of the game is to make trouble for the opponents. For example, opening a weak two in any position with a five-card major and some shape is very popular today among experts. The argument in favor goes like this.

> **"If the opponents are experienced players, they will have a rough time guessing what to do - inexperienced players will be lost."**
> **- Eddie Kantar**

To illustrate the degree of preempting today, an expert would not hesitate to preempt, not vulnerable, with any of the following hands.

Modern Day Preempts

♠KQJ96 ♥72 ♦10542 ♣87   — 2S

♠42 ♥65 ♦1086 ♣QJ10963   — 3C

♠64 ♥J872 ♦QJ1094 ♣62   — 2D

Figure 2-2

True, there are risks associated with these kinds of preemptive bids. But in the first case above, if you can get the lead of that suit a near top board is possible. In all three cases, the opponents will have to guess; they may reach the wrong strain or the wrong level or both.

The only real restraints experts have on preempts today is defensive strength. Even that restraint is relaxed if partner has passed and your hand is minor-suit oriented or you are missing the all-important **boss spade suit**. Once in a while a preempt backfires and you will go for a big number. However, you never know in advance what's going to happen and more often than not the preempt will pay off. So, do it consistently and philosophically accept the occasional bad result along with the many good ones.

Open Light Hands

The next way experts get their bid in early is by opening light hands. They will open hands with high card strength ranging from 8 - 11 points as long as the hand has shape, controls (aces/stiffs) and the high cards are in the long suits. (See Figure 2-3.)

Light Opening Bids

```
♠AQ64  ♥72  ♦54  ♣KQ875

♠KQ8642  ♥A9872  ♦8  ♣4

♠6  ♥AJ10953  ♦KQ8  ♣542
```

Figure 2-3

As to garbage-type 11-12 point balanced hands, there is no consensus among experts. Some open them and others either pass or reserve this type of hand for a weak notrump bid. Take your choice. Some experts from the old school still insist on very sound opening bids - but they haven't won any events in the past decade. All of today's top pairs play aggressive (light) opening bids, takeout doubles and overcalls.

Make Light Takeout Doubles

Light takeout doubles are a universally accepted way to get your bid in early. The rule is the better the shape, the less the high card requirements. You can have as few as 9 or 10 points or even less as a passed hand. If your right-hand opponent opens one club, for example, the hands in Figure 2-4 all qualify for a light takeout double.

Light Takeout Doubles

♠A752 ♥K976 ♦Q432 ♣7

♠A873 ♥K95 ♦A1065 ♣85

♠KQ97 ♥J85 ♦J1084 ♣A6

Figure 2-4

Notice that in the last two cases the takeout double can result in a 4-3 fit. Experts don't mind playing 4-3 fits in major suits. In fact at matchpoints they prefer to do so, especially in partscore contracts, for several reasons. A major suit:

- Maximizes your scoring potential.
- Allows you to play a lower level contract.
- Allows you to push the opponents up an extra level and possibly defeat them.
- Allows you to sacrifice for a smaller loss.

Make Light Overcalls

The last way to get your bid in early is through the overcall and there are several options: overcalling a suit, preempting or making a two-suited overcall. If you have two suits, the modern trend is toward getting them both in because the next time around the auction may be at the 4 or 5 level. Two-suited bids as well as mere overcalls open up the possibility of a partscore, a game contract, a sacrifice, or a lead director - any one of which could earn you a good result.

The experts today consider the 1 level a "free lunch." Almost never are these 1-level bids doubled for penalties so it is worth the risk to get your bid in. The experts will make overcalls on almost anything; for example, ♠KJ10xx and nothing else. At the very least, they want the lead of that suit in case the opponents reach a notrump contract.

Some experts will also overcall four-card suits at the 1 level. There are several requirements: (1) the suit must be decent, (2) more total high-card values are needed to make up for the short suit, and (3) the hand should not otherwise qualify for a takeout double or a notrump overcall. All of these four-card suits in Figure 2-5 would qualify.

4-Card Overcalls

```
KJ107

AJ106

AK98

AQ105
```

Figure 2-5

Like regular overcalls these four-card suits can lead to excellent opening leads on defense, or to competition for a partscore contract, or to a preemptive, disrupting bid, or to a game contract. Another advantage of more flexible initial overcalls is that they minimize the risk of taking unwise balancing actions at higher levels (see page 14).

BE AGGRESSIVE ON CONTESTED AUCTIONS

On contested auctions there can be quick entry into the bidding as we have seen through light opening bids, preempts, overcalls and takeout doubles. There can also be quick exits if partner shows no interest, or there can be fiercely fought partscore battles. The objective of these battles is threefold: (1) take the contract and go plus or (2) be minus less than the opponents would have otherwise scored or (3) jack the opponents up another level and go plus.

In partscore skirmishes the rule is **do not let the opponents play anything at the 2 level if they have a fit**. As soon as your side has found its own fit, the further rule is to **go to your combined trump level immediately** in order to (1) take space from the opponents and (2) help partner set the maximum level of your contract.

The Law Controls The Level

The generally accepted guide for controlling the level of the auction in competitive bidding is the "Law of Total Tricks." In essence you should always bid to the level equal to the combined number of trumps held by your side. When your side has eight trumps you can safely bid to the two level; if your side has nine trumps you can safely bid to the three level.

> **"Even if you go down, you'll be sacrificing against whatever the opponents can make."**   **- Larry Cohen**

While experts often will bid up to their level of combined trumps, they may bid one more or less depending on hand evaluation. For example, more conservative action is called for when your hand is flat and contains soft values in side suits or queens and jacks in the opponents' suits. More aggressive action is called for when your hand has good shape, hard values, no wasted values in opponents' suits or a great fit. Figure 2-6 highlights these hand evaluation factors which might adjust your contract level up or down **one** trick.*

---

*For further explanation, see <u>To Bid or Not to Bid - The Law of Total Tricks</u>, Cohen.

Adjusting the Law of Total Tricks Up or Down One Trick

HAND EVALUATION	UP	DOWN
1. Shape:		
• Flat		X
• Distributional	X	
2. Long trump suit	X	
3. Soft values - Queens, Jacks:		
• In short side suits		X
• In opponents' suits		X
• In your trump suit	X	
4. Hard Values - Aces, Kings	X	
5. Degree of fit:		
• Misfit		X
• Super fit	X	
• Double fit	X	

Figure 2-6

Take Partscore Sacrifices

Once the partscore auction is underway, there is always the issue of whether you should sacrifice. Good matchpoint scores can be had by going minus 50 or 100 instead of allowing the opponents to score plus 110 or 140. Experts frequently will take the partscore sacrifice, even vulnerable, and take the chance that the opponents will not double them. The 3 level is usually the limit in partscore sacrifices although distribution and great fits can justify exceptions.

Don't Take the Push Easily - Use the Law

Don't take the push easily in these partscore wars (you don't want to get the reputation as being easy to "push around"). If you do, good players will never let you play the contract (unless you are going minus). Even good players get overzealous in this area and bid too much. The solution is to let the Law of Total Tricks guide you to the appropriate level.

If the opponents continue to bid, you should defend. If it seems to be your hand and the opponents are pushing you around, you should double. This is a cooperative double, a weapon devised by experts to combat aggressive opponents and to help make these close decisions on a partnership basis. The double allows partner to consider such things as his own trump length and distribution before either agreeing to the double or bidding one more. This system works beautifully! (For further discussion of cooperative doubles see page 239.)

BE DISCIPLINED ON UNCONTESTED AUCTIONS

At matchpoints, experts take the middle of the road on games and slams. They bid the obvious ones but do not push for the borderline ones, unless there is a super or double fit. It is okay to be optimistic when all of your values are working and your shortness is in the right suits, but partnerships can not always uncover such perfect fits. So the experts play the odds and bid both games and slams that are obvious but let the others go. The argument goes this way. Being out of step with the field may cost a near bottom, while following the field allows the expert to pick up an extra trick in the play of the hand and still achieve a well above average result on the board.

Accordingly experts do not stretch in an attempt to reach close games or slams or use the much-abused Blackwood convention to explore slams (see page 241). Instead, experts use such things as game and slam tries to explore the limits of partner's hand. As one of them put it,

> "Do not try to make your partner's decisions for him. Give him a chance to stop below game if he has a minimum hand. Stretching or pressing can result only in poor matchpoint scores."   - Hugh Kelsey

BE CONSERVATIVE ON MISFITS

The objective of experts in misfit situations is to cut your losses and go minus as little as possible or allow the opponents to play the hand (and let them go minus). On misfits, experts have learned the hard way to make the tough decisions - bail out quickly and don't fight partner for the contract. It only produces bad results and insults partner. For example:

South
♠ —
♥ KJ96543
♦ AJ8
♣ K97

West	North	East	South
			1♥
Pass	1♠	Pass	2♥
Pass	2♠	Pass	?

Pass and leave well enough alone.

Trying to find a better contract can be expensive. First, it forces the level of bidding up and thus the number of tricks required; secondly, it invites a penalty double from the opponents - something they may have been unwilling to do at a lower level. Unfortunately, real values are required to bid and find the right contract. If you bid without values in an effort to better place the contract, partner will not know the difference between those bids and others that seek a game or slam. And so continued bidding only invites disaster.

Frequently, misfit situations exist on both sides of the table. The expert strategy in misfits is to close off the bidding quickly, hoping that the opponents will jump into the fire. If they do, the expert will settle for a plus or double to cut off any further bidding from his partner (sometimes referred to as the "shutup double"). At least, if partner does any further bidding he will have to do so *entirely* on his own.

BALANCING IS A DISCRETE BUSINESS

The expert's approach to balancing is very simple - **don't** by getting your bid in early. This eliminates the need to stick your head into the auction later on and possibly get it chopped off. When getting your bid in early is not possible, experts will balance freely on fit auctions. This is done on the grounds that *if the opponents have a fit, you have a fit*.

> "On those sequences where your opponents have shown a fit and limited values, your attitude toward reopening should range from strongly inclined to obsessive. It is almost inexcusable to allow your opponents to play at the 2 level when they want to do so."   - Mike Lawrence

Whoever is **short** in the opponents' suit, whether in direct seat or pass out seat, is the designated balancer. If that person does not act, his partner with length in the opponents' suit will usually pass out the auction. The person who acts does not necessarily need much in the way of values, only some shape and shortness in the opponents' suit. As the balancer, he is in fact bidding his partner's values. The reopening bid is usually made in one of three ways: (1) a takeout double or (2) bidding an unbid suit or (3) bidding 2NT for the minors.

If, on the other hand, the auction suggests a misfit, experts will use extreme caution and will not enter the auction without a good suit of their own. How do you know there is a misfit? Usually the auction ends with the opponents taking a mere preference or bidding 1NT. In these kinds of auctions, the opponents are bidding on high cards rather than fits. To illustrate:

West	North	East	South
Pass	1♦	Pass	1♥
Pass	1♠	Pass	1NT
Pass	Pass	?	

The opponents have a misfit, but with the majority of the high cards they would love to double you if they get a chance! Further, when the opponents have no fit there is no reason to believe that you have one.

Therefore, when reopening in a suit, experts give special attention to the "safe suit/dangerous suit" concept.* For example, dangerous suits are ones which are underneath the opener's suit or ones that the responder may have skipped over or did not have the opportunity to bid.

Dangerous/Safe Suit Concept

Auctions		Dangerous Suits	Safe Suits
1. 1♠ 1NT 2♦ P		Clubs Hearts	None
2. 1♣ 1♠ 1NT P		Hearts Diamonds	None
3. 1♦ 1♥ 1NT P		Clubs Spades	None
4. P 1♥ 1NT P		Diamonds Clubs	Spades
5. 1♣ 1♥ 1NT P		Spades Diamonds	None

Figure 2-7

In the first auction above, responder did not have the opportunity to bid either clubs or hearts, so both are dangerous. Since responder is extremely short in spades (and partner is long in spades), you are probably walking into a hornet's nest in this auction. The same kinds of dangers are in auctions 2 and 3. For example, in auction 2 opener could not bid hearts

---

*The Complete Book on Balancing, Lawrence, page 46.

and responder may have skipped over diamonds in favor of bidding the major suit, spades. Only in auction 4 do we find a safe suit, spades, because both opener and responder had the opportunity to bid them but did not.

Generally speaking, experts get their bids in earlier at the 1 level. When they do reopen the bidding at the 2 level or higher on misfit auctions, it is premised on either a good suit or a higher ranking (safe) suit which the opponents had the opportunity to bid and did not.

FAVOR NOTRUMP FIRST, MAJOR SUITS NEXT, MINOR SUITS LAST

Matchpoint scoring puts a premium on notrump and major suit contracts. Therefore, it is generally understood that (1) all balanced hands without major suit fits will play best in *notrump* and (2) good major-suit fits will usually play best in a *major-suit* contract. However, experts have additional guidelines as to when they do and do not play in these premium contracts (see Figure 2-8).

Guidelines for Deciding Premium Contracts

Favor Notrump When You Have:	Favor Major Suit When You Have:
• Minor-suit fits	• Good fits
• Misfit hands	• Slow tricks
• Fast tricks, solid suits	• Good 5-2 or 5-3 fits, if a side suit too weak for notrump
• Overpowered balanced hands (29-31 points)	• 4-3 fits if: - Your short trump side can stop the force
• Weak major-suit fits	- You have minor-suit fit on the side
• 5-2 and 5-3 major-suit fits, if other suits well stopped	
• Flat (4-3-3-3) distribution	

Figure 2-8

Most of these guidelines are obvious to you but a few require comment. Long solid suits, even in the majors, are good candidates for notrump contracts if the rest of the hand contains fast tricks. Major-suit fits with values just short of slam (29-31 points) are also candidates for notrump contracts because all suits will be well stopped. All hands with 4-3-3-3 flat distribution are excellent candidates for notrumps, **even** those with 5-4 major-suit fits.

As to major-suit contracts, most neglected are those with 4-3 fits. There are two useful conditions for these kinds of contracts: (1) a good minor suit fit on the side as a source of tricks (and, if need be, to force the opponents out of trumps) and (2) shortness in the opponents' strong suit on the short trump side to keep the opponents from forcing you out of trumps. When these conditions are present, a near top board will be the result.

SACRIFICE OFTEN AT GAME AND SLAM LEVELS

Sacrificing in matchpoints is a way of waging war against the opponents' game and slam contracts - especially under favorable vulnerability conditions. Matchpoint scoring allows a great deal of leeway in sacrificing. So, experts give considerable emphasis to sacrificing when the opponents have reached a reasonably sure game or slam contract. A good board can result in two different ways. The first is obvious - by being minus less than the opponents' game or slam contract is worth. The second way you can get a good result is for the opponents to take the push to the next level and go minus.

How do the experts make these difficult kinds of decisions on sacrifices? The general criteria are as follows:

- Great fits and distribution (the more the better at higher levels)
- Controls (singletons, voids and aces)
- Little defense against the opponents' contract.

In acting on these criteria, the partner with little or no defense (the weaker hand) usually defers to the other partner for a final decision.

As we bring this chapter on matchpoint bidding to a close, there are several things to keep in mind:

- Put your bidding shoes on and keep them on.
- Remember, the one who gets information to partner first wins.
- Interfere as much as you can with the opponents and make their communications difficult, if not impossible.

> **"Fear should not deter you from bidding. Winning bridge is the result of being aggressive and fighting for what is yours."**
> **- Mike Lawrence**

− − − − − −

In matchpoints certain decisions are made during the course of the bidding, and it is important to back up these decisions, whether right or wrong, in the play of the hand. The next chapter prepares you for this task. But, before you take on Chapter 3, see if you can pass the quiz on this one.

QUIZ FOR CHAPTER 2

The answers to these problems begin on page 27. If you get 90% of them right you can hold your own with the experts. If you answer 75% correctly you are making good progress toward your goal, but if you get only 50% right, perhaps you should study this chapter again.

1.　　You are West. What do you bid on each of the following hands at equal vulnerability?

a)　　♠AQ1064　♥3　♦Q752　♣853

West	North	East	South
?			

b)　　♠KJ107652　♥__　♦63　♣QJ85

West	North	East	South
		Pass	Pass
?			

c)　　♠8　♥652　♦AJ10852　♣KQ7

West	North	East	South
		Pass	Pass
?			

d)　　♠K742　♥6　♦3　♣KQ109742

West	North	East	South
			Pass
?			

e)   ♠Q5 ♥K43 ♦A109753 ♣J6

West	North	East	South
			Pass
?			

f)   ♠64 ♥Q7 ♦AQJ1084 ♣Q106

West	North	East	South
?			

g)   ♠Q76 ♥42 ♦8743 ♣A652

West	North	East	South
		3♠	Pass
?			

2.   You are South. What do you do with each of the following hands, not vulnerable?

a)   ♠93 ♥AJ1074 ♦10842 ♣62

West	North	East	South
Pass	Pass	1♦	?

b)   ♠A1082   ♥KJ ♦J752 ♣K76

West	North	East	South
	Pass	1♣	?

c)   ♠KQ106   ♥64 ♦Q7632 ♣85

West	North	East	South
Pass	Pass	1♦	?

d) ♠AJ9743 ♥7 ♦84 ♣J1064

West	North	East	South
Pass	Pass	1♣	?

e) ♠AJ107 ♥4 ♦KJ42 ♣QJ76

West	North	East	South
		1♦	?

f) ♠KJ1094 ♥62 ♦73 ♣K1084

West	North	East	South
	Pass	1♦	?

3.   You are South in these contested auctions. It is your bid with no one vulnerable.

a)   ♠Q64 ♥AJ105 ♦J1094 ♣AJ

West	North	East	South
			1♦
Double	1♠	2♣	?

b)   ♠J9742 ♥A3 ♦KQ107 ♣Q4

West	North	East	South
			1♠
Double	2♠	3♣	?

c)   ♠KJ104 ♥64 ♦A10732 ♣J10

West	North	East	South
1♥	Pass	2♥	?

d) ♠J1084 ♥3 ♦A1073 ♣J743

West	North	East	South
1♦	1♠	Pass	?

e) ♠KQ104 ♥J972 ♦K73 ♣32

West	North	East	South
1♥	Pass	2♥	?

4. On the following auctions, you are South with both sides vulnerable. What is your bid?

a) ♠6 ♥94 ♦J42 ♣KJ97632

West	North	East	South
	1♠	Pass	?

b) ♠J ♥KQ7432 ♦J76 ♣J84

West	North	East	South
Pass	1♠	Pass	1NT
Pass	2♠	Pass	?

c) ♠76 ♥Q1076 ♦A73 ♣K1053

West	North	East	South
	1♠	Pass	1NT
Pass	2♦	Pass	?

d) ♠J4 ♥8 ♦K10765 ♣J8642

West	North	East	South
	1♥	Pass	?

e)   ♠1087 ♥4 ♦K752 ♣Q6432

West	North	East	South
	1♥	Pass	?

f)   ♠K4 ♥KQ9874 ♦AK ♣A73

West	North	East	South
			1♥
1♠	Pass	Pass	Double
2♠	Pass	Pass	?

g)   ♠5 ♥KQJ3 ♦KQ865 ♣KQJ

West	North	East	South
	3♠	Pass	?

5.   In the following auctions, you are West with equal vulnerability.
Do you contest or pass?

a)   ♠108765 ♥4 ♦Q63 ♣AJ65

West	North	East	South
			1♥
Pass	2♥	Pass	Pass
?			

b)   ♠KJ6 ♥Q742 ♦K753 ♣84

West	North	East	South
Pass	1♣	Pass	2♣
?			

c) ♠Q1073 ♥643 ♦K6 ♣A1054

West	North	East	South
			1♥
Pass	2♥	Pass	Pass
?			

d) ♠63 ♥52 ♦AQ106 ♣QJ974

West	North	East	South
	1♠	Pass	2♠
?			

e) ♠K4 ♥742 ♦Q4 ♣AQ7653

West	North	East	South
	1♥	Pass	1NT
Pass	2♦	Pass	Pass
?			

f) ♠AK75 ♥K742 ♦K65 ♣108

West	North	East	South
	1♦	Pass	1♠
Pass	1NT	Pass	Pass
?			

6. You are South on the 6 auctions below. What do you favor as a final contract in each case - notrump, a major suit, or a minor suit?

a) ♠6 ♥A2 ♦AKQJ1075 ♣843

West	North	East	South
	Pass	1♠	?

b)   ♠KQ   ♥AQ73   ♦Q42   ♣J652

West	North	East	South
	1NT	Pass	?

c)   ♠AJ4   ♥K72   ♦96   ♣KQ742

West	North	East	South
		Pass	1♣
Pass	1♠	Pass	1NT
Pass	3♣[1]	Pass	?

[1]Invitational

d)   ♠K942   ♥J64   ♦K53   ♣AJ7

West	North	East	South
	1♠	Pass	2NT[1]
Pass	3NT	Pass	?

[1]Strong spade raise

e)   ♠KQ97   ♥10742   ♦AJ4   ♣J3

West	North	East	South
	1♣	Pass	1♥
Pass	2♥	Pass	?

ANSWERS TO CHAPTER 2 QUIZ

1. You are West. What do you bid on each of the following hands at equal vulnerability?

   a) ♠AQ1064 ♥3 ♦Q752 ♣853

West	North	East	South
?			

   Bid two spades. That's the lead you want if the opponents have the balance of power. If it is their hand, they will have to guess what to do. If, on the other hand, your partner has game going values, he can inquire as to your hand quality and trump length and set the final contract accordingly.

   b) ♠KJ107652 ♥__ ♦63 ♣QJ85

West	North	East	South
		Pass	Pass
?			

   Bid four spades, the toughest bid in bridge to contend with. The odds are that the opponents have a game in hearts, diamonds, or notrump. If the person in fourth position has a strong hand, he will have to guess what to do. If the opponents' values are divided, the chances are you will not be doubled.

   c) ♠8 ♥652 ♦AJ10852 ♣KQ7

West	North	East	South
		Pass	Pass
?			

   Bid three diamonds. True, you have a great hand but chances are the opponents have a partscore or game in one of the majors, and you will be **outbid**. Partner is a passed hand, so you will not miss game.

d) ♠K742 ♥6 ♦3 ♣KQ109742

West	North	East	South
			Pass
?			

Pass. If your partner has the boss suit, spades, you may have a partscore or game in that strain. Preempting three clubs could eliminate a superior contract.

e) ♠Q5 ♥K43 ♦A109753 ♣J6

West	North	East	South
			Pass
?			

Pass. You have too much defense against any contract the opponents might bid. No reason to preempt partner.

f) ♠64 ♥Q7 ♦AQJ1084 ♣Q106

West	North	East	South
?			

Bid one diamond. Your suit is so outstanding you might miss a game or slam if you preempt. (As third hand, bid 3 diamonds.)

g) ♠Q76 ♥42 ♦8743 ♣A652

West	North	East	South
		3♠	Pass
?			

Bid four spades! The opponents are cold for a game. Don't let the opponents exchange information. If you wait and then sacrifice, the opponents will know you have a weak hand. Cloud the issue and make them guess.

2. You are South. What do you do with each of the following hands, not vulnerable?

a) ♠93 ♥AJ1074 ♦10842 ♣62

West	North	East	South
Pass	Pass	1♦	?

Bid one heart, as a lead director, or two hearts preemptive. After hearing your bid, however, partner may have sufficient values to compete for a partscore or take space from the opponents by preempting.

b) ♠A1082 ♥KJ ♦J752 ♣K76

West	North	East	South
	Pass	1♣	?

Pass. This is your typical balanced, garbage hand with no suit. Partner will bid hearts if you double and you'll play in a 4-2 fit. You may be able to reopen the bidding later with a double if the opponents bid hearts.

c) ♠KQ106 ♥64 ♦Q7632 ♣85

West	North	East	South
Pass	Pass	1♦	?

Bid one spade and pass at your next opportunity. As your partner surely is short in diamonds, he is likely to have some length in spades. He may be able to compete for a partscore or steal space from the opponents by preempting.

d) ♠AJ9743 ♥7 ♦84 ♣J1064

West	North	East	South
Pass	Pass	1♣	?

Bid two spades (or three spades if you are feeling frisky). The opponents have the balance of power; put them on the guess.

e)   ♠AJ107   ♥4   ♦KJ42   ♣QJ76

West	North	East	South
		1♦	?

Bid one spade. Pass might work if the auction permits you to come in later. If partner supports spades fine; if he bids hearts and the opponents continue bidding, you can double them. If the opponents stay quiet, you can settle for notrump.

f)   ♠KJ1094   ♥62   ♦73   ♣K1084

West	North	East	South
	Pass	1♦	?

Bid two spades. Make it as difficult as you can for the opponents.

3.   You are South in these contested auctions. It is your bid with no one vulnerable.

a)   ♠Q64   ♥AJ105   ♦J1094   ♣AJ

West	North	East	South
			1♦
Double	1♠	2♣	?

Bid two spades, or double if you use support doubles. The opponents likely have a club fit, and you should not allow them to play it at the 2 level.

b)   ♠J9742   ♥A3   ♦KQ107   ♣Q4

West	North	East	South
			1♠
Double	2♠	3♣	?

Pass. You have reached the level of your combined trumps - the Law of Total Tricks. If partner had 4 trumps, he would have gone to 3 spades immediately or made some stronger bid. Some of your values are not working (♣Q) and your trump suit is weak. Bidding further clearly violates the law. If you did, bail has been set for $10,000. Good luck!

c)   ♠KJ104   ♥64   ♦A10732   ♣J10

West	North	East	South
1♥	Pass	2♥	?

Bid two spades. If you double, you don't want to hear 3 clubs. The worst case is probably a 4-3 spade fit. You are short in the opponents' suit and therefore must take action. If they have a fit, you have a fit.

d)   ♠J1084   ♥3   ♦A1073   ♣J743

West	North	East	South
1♦	1♠	Pass	?

Bid three diamonds - what the experts refer to as a "mixed raise." Your hand is too strong for a preemptive bid but not strong enough for a limit raise. If you did not have the diamond ace, the expert bid would be three spades, preemptive. Your objective here is to steal some space from the opponents and at the same time show support for partner.

e)   ♠KQ104   ♥J972   ♦K73   ♣32

West	North	East	South
1♥	Pass	2♥	?

Pass. Partner has shortness in the opponent's heart suit and should certainly reopen if the auction is about to be passed out. In balancing position, he is entitled to bid your hand. If you bid now, partner could interpret your bid as a stronger hand than you actually have.

4. On the following auctions, you are South with both sides vulnerable. What is your bid?

a) ♠6 ♥94 ♦J42 ♣KJ97632

West	North	East	South
	1♠	Pass	?

Pass or three clubs, if you play that bid as a weak jump shift. There is risk associated with a 1NT bid because a misfit is likely and you will be unhappy with partner's next bid. If the auction permits, however, come in later with your club suit. Partner will know your hand has value only if played in clubs.

b) ♠J ♥KQ7432 ♦J76 ♣J84

West	North	East	South
Pass	1♠	Pass	1NT
Pass	2♠	Pass	?

Pass. Your 8 points do not justify another bid, especially in view of the misfit. Hearts may be a better contract but you need values (not dreams) to find out.

c) ♠76 ♥Q1076 ♦A73 ♣K1053

West	North	East	South
	1♠	Pass	1NT
Pass	2♦	Pass	?

Bid two spades. Don't make the mistake of bidding 2NT on this misfit. Your hand is worth a preference bid only. If partner takes another bid you can respond positively.

d) ♠J4 ♥8 ♦K10765 ♣J8642

West	North	East	South
	1♥	Pass	?

Pass. You don't want to hear the next bid - more than likely it will be two or three hearts.

e) ♠1087 ♥4 ♦K752 ♣Q6432

West	North	East	South
	1♥	Pass	?

Pass. There may be a better place to play but first let's hear from the opponents. You may have something further to say later depending on how the auction goes. If you do, partner will know you have a misfit and limited values.

f) ♠K4 ♥KQ9874 ♦AK ♣A73

West	North	East	South
			1♥
1♠	Pass	Pass	Double
2♠	Pass	Pass	?

Double (cooperative). Partner passed twice and will know what to do. It turns out that partner was void in hearts (his reason for passing your opening bid) and will be happy to pass again for a 2-trick set. Three hearts goes down one for a minus score. If partner had a couple of hearts and no defense against the spade contract, he would simply bid three hearts.

g) ♠5 ♥KQJ3 ♦KQ865 ♣KQJ

West	North	East	South
	3♠	Pass	?

Pass. Even though you have 17 points, don't bid 3NT. Nine tricks are next to impossible opposite a spade-oriented hand and limited entries. Notrump games with misfits require 2 things: (1) several points more than normal and (2) transportation between the two hands.

5. In the following auctions, you are West with equal vulnerability. Do you contest or pass?

a)   ♠108765 ♥4 ♦Q63 ♣AJ65

West	North	East	South
			1♥
Pass	2♥	Pass	Pass
?			

Bid two spades. This is a "safe" suit and in balancing position you can bid your partner's values. Partner obviously has close to an opening bid but not enough shape to come in on his own. You may not buy the contract but jacking the opponents up just one level higher will improve your chances of beating them.

b)   ♠KJ6 ♥Q742 ♦K753 ♣84

West	North	East	South
Pass	1♣	Pass	2♣
?			

Double. You have the shape and tolerance for the unbid suits. A 4-3 spade fit will work because you can ruff clubs in the short hand.

c)   ♠Q1073 ♥643 ♦K6 ♣A1054

West	North	East	South
			1♥
Pass	2♥	Pass	Pass
?			

Double or bid two spades - a relatively safe suit. If the opponents have a fit, so do you. You are willing to play in a 4-3 fit at the 2 level, if necessary.

d)   ♠63 ♥52 ♦AQ106 ♣QJ974

West	North	East	South
	1♠	Pass	2♠
?			

Bid 2NT, hoping to find partner with a 4-card minor. There is a reasonable chance of this because partner could not overcall hearts but could have as much as 10 points. Don't let them play at the 2 level with a fit. And, if they have a fit so do you.

e)   ♠K4 ♥742 ♦Q4 ♣AQ7653

West	North	East	South
	1♥	Pass	1NT
Pass	2♦	Pass	Pass
?			

Pass. As in many misfit auctions, let the opponents play it. The one notrumper just took a preference; he likes hearts even less than diamonds (stiff or void) and can't have spades. Guess what he likes? Your clubs are a dangerous suit and lack the spots you need to go to the 3 level by yourself.

f)   ♠AK75 ♥K742 ♦K65 ♣108

West	North	East	South
	1♦	Pass	1♠
Pass	1NT	Pass	Pass
?			

Pass. North could have bid clubs but did not. He probably has hearts but lacked the values to bid them over his partner's spade response. So, you have *their* suits. Partner has clubs. Best you go quietly.

6.   You are South on the 6 auctions below. What do you favor as a final contract in each case - notrump, a major suit, or a minor suit?

a)   ♠6 ♥A2 ♦AKQJ1075 ♣843

West	North	East	South
	Pass	1♠	?

Bid three spades, asking partner to bid 3NT if he has a spade stopper. If he does not, he will correct to four clubs and you will further correct to diamonds. Meanwhile, you have explored your best matchpoint option for a final contract and at the same time you have severely disrupted the opponents' bidding.

b) ♠KQ ♥AQ73 ♦Q42 ♣J652

West	North	East	South
	1NT	Pass	?

Bid 3NT. You have a combined total of from 29 to 31 points. You are overpowered for four hearts but are too weak for slam. Your short suit values offset the need for ruffing power. Further, you can often pick up an extra trick in notrump contracts on the opening lead. Although there is no guarantee, go for the best matchpoint score.

c) ♠AJ4 ♥K72 ♦96 ♣KQ742

West	North	East	South
		Pass	1♣
Pass	1♠	Pass	1NT
Pass	3♣[1]	Pass	?

[1]Invitational

Bid three spades inviting partner to four if he has a decent suit. With wonderful 3-card spade support, there is a good chance for game. The short hand can ruff the third diamond and clubs will run.

d) ♠K942 ♥J64 ♦K53 ♣AJ7

West	North	East	South
	1♠	Pass	2NT[1]
Pass	3NT	Pass	?

[1]Strong spade raise

Pass. Partner shows a balanced hand and opening notrump values. Despite a 5-4 spade fit, you have no ruffing power. Go for your extra 10 points at matchpoints.

e)   ♠KQ97 ♥10742 ♦AJ4 ♣J3

West	North	East	South
	1♣	Pass	1♥
Pass	2♥	Pass	?

Bid 2NT, inviting game in either hearts or notrump. Your values are outside the heart suit which is weak and the unbid suits are double stopped. In addition, notrump contracts may produce an extra trick because they are difficult to defend against. Go for a near top but let partner share in this key decision.

Chapter 3

HOW EXPERTS PLAY HANDS AT MATCHPOINTS*

Declarer play at matchpoints must keep faith with the final contract, no matter how good or how bad the contract is. As soon as the dummy appears, the expert assesses whether the contract is a **normal, ideal** or **poor** one. The answer can have a profound effect on how he plays the hand.

In any total-point form of scoring, such as teams, making the contract is all-important. Overtricks are of minor significance. In matchpoints, however, the situation is just the opposite. The tendency is away from safety and toward taking risk for overtricks. In an effort to go plus more than the other pairs, experts will take risks which would be unthinkable in total-point scoring.

Matchpoint declarer play, however, is not just a matter of overtricks. Certain matchpoint decisions have been made during the course of the bidding and it is important to back up these decisions, whether good or bad, in the play of the hand. In other words, the expert adopts a line of play consistent with his bidding. It is called the "keep faith" concept.

While keeping a poker face, the first thing the expert does when dummy hits the table is evaluate the contract, comparing it with contracts likely to be reached at other tables (the field). On a few occasions the expert will have missed an obvious game or bid too strongly and landed in a seemingly impossible contract. Or he may have reached the right level

---

*To achieve expert status in card play technique itself requires much knowledge of and experience with such things as card reading, suit combinations, percentages, trump management, dummy reversals, end plays and squeezes. Such knowledge and experience is something each person must acquire on his own over time. The literature is rich in card-play technique and there are good computer programs today which will challenge your expertise. Chapter 10 identifies the great classics on card play technique as well as computer programs to practice your declarer play.

but the wrong contract. In such cases, he is doomed to a very poor score. The only hope is to keep faith with his bidding and adjust his declarer play accordingly.

NORMAL CONTRACTS

In *normal* contracts, experts take any reasonable risk for overtricks, including risks which might even jeopardize the contract. Reasonable risk is when you are favored to take the trick - that is, the odds or percentages are in your favor. Further, safety plays are not taken on *normal* contracts. To illustrate:

Contract: 3NT	♠642
Lead: ♣5	♥976
	♦AKQ73
	♣32

♠AKQ
♥AQ3
♦864
♣A1064

In this case the expert would play for the odds-on 3-2 break and go for all 5 tricks. In the event diamonds broke badly for him (4-1), the expert's contract would be in serious jeopardy. But this is the nature of matchpoints - you must try to beat the other pairs when the odds are in your favor.

If the expert had one less diamond in the South hand (seven of them), he would duck the first diamond to the defenders. This is not a safety play. Rather, the expert is just playing the odds that the diamonds don't figure to break 3-3 the majority of the time.*

So in *normal* matchpoint contracts, play the odds and do it consistently. As your decisions will be right most of the time, it will be easier (philosophically) to accept a bad result once in a while.

---

*Generally speaking, the percentages are that an odd number of outstanding cards will break for declarer and an even number of outstanding cards will not break for declarer.

IDEAL CONTRACTS

Ideal contracts are easy to handle. Simply disregard overtricks and play the hand safely. Merely making a magnificent contract is enough to get most of the matchpoints. For example:

Contract: 2H	♠6
Lead: ♠A	♥532
Switch: ♥J	♦AQJ853
	♣J76

```
            ♠J1042
            ♥AKQ7
            ♦K4
            ♣Q84
```

After the defender takes his spade ace, he switches to the heart jack to cut down declarer's ruffing power. What is your play?

When the dummy goes down, the expert sees that most of the field will be either in diamonds, making plus 110 or 130, or in notrump, making plus 120. So, if he can score at least 140, he will get most of the matchpoints. Accordingly, the expert will duck the ♥J as a safety play to counter the expected (odds-on) 4-2 break in trumps.

The safety play ensures 9 tricks and more if the defenders do not cash out right away. If the declarer does not make the safety play in trumps, he will lose control of the hand to a defender who has 4 trumps.

POOR CONTRACTS

Poor contracts are a different matter; when you are in a bad contract you are destined for a zero (or near zero). *Poor* contracts present an overwhelming challenge to declarer play and obviously should be avoided (unless you are trying to improve your declarer play).

The expert first determines where the field is going to be on the deal and what that score will be and then plays the cards for an equal or better score, if he can. If a miracle or some unusual distribution or lie of the cards is required, that's how the hand should be played. There is really very little risk - your matchpoint score can only go up. Figure 3-1 shows the types of *poor* contracts you might encounter (or preferably watch your opponents encounter) at matchpoints and what should be done to alter declarer play.

Poor Matchpoint Contracts

Reason for Poor Contract	What Should be Done During Declarer Play
Underbid	Assume bad lie of cards (even if odds are against you)
Overbid	Assume good lie of cards (even if odds are against you)
Abnormal Contract	Play to outscore normal contract

Figure 3-1

Let's take a look at how to approach the declarer play on several of these *poor* contracts:

Underbid Contracts

Contract: 3C	♠J96
Lead: ♥2	♥A1053
	♦QJ74
	♣94

♠AK
♥762
♦105
♣AKQ1063

The dummy comes down and you analyze that the field will be in 3NT on this hand. How do you think the expert will play the hand?

If the clubs behave normally, the field will make 3NT and the expert is destined for a near bottom board. The only chance he has of salvaging some matchpoints on the board is to assume (worst case) that East has 4 clubs to the Jack which will leave the 3 notrumpers short one trick. Accordingly, he will take the club finesse and if his pessimistic view turns out to be right, he will be plus 110 and the field will be minus 50. If the pessimistic view is wrong, an already poor result will only be slightly worse.

Overbid Contracts

On the other hand if the expert overbids a particular hand, he takes just the opposite approach - he views things optimistically and plays for suits to break favorably, despite the odds. We need no examples here - we've all had lots of experience with getting too high on contracts! Once you are there make the best of it and assume a favorable lie of the cards. Don't ever give up - miracles do happen! And, don't worry about going down an extra trick - your score can't get much worse than it already is.

Abnormal Contracts

```
Contract: 3NT          ♠742
Lead: ♠5               ♥8653
                       ♦A972
                       ♣AJ


                       ♠KQ
                       ♥AKQ72
                       ♦K83
                       ♣K75
```

West	North	East	South
	Pass	Pass	2NT
Pass	3NT	(All pass)	

The dummy appears and you see that your partner was a little overzealous in bidding 3NT since the field will be in 4H, making 5. After the attacking spade lead, how do you think the expert will play this hand?

He will finesse the ♣J and jeopardize the contract! If it works, he makes 5 NT for a top score. If not, he loses very little. Plus 430 will be a near zero.

OTHER FACTORS INFLUENCING DECLARER PLAY

There are a couple of other factors that can influence declarer play in matchpoints. If the defender makes a lucky or killing lead, the expert will take more chances than normal in order to recover the lost ground. He already has a poor result, so the risk is not that great. On the other hand, if the expert receives a favorable lead, he will retain the edge over the field and keep risk in declarer play to a minimum.

In partscore battles, it is not unusual for experts to take sacrifices when their opponents can score, for example, 110 or 140. In these situations, experts will make safety plays, if necessary, to assure that their loss is less than their opponents gain would have been.

In conclusion, the important thing is to compare your contract (after all, you are stuck with it) to the field's expected result and adjust your declarer play accordingly, always keeping faith with your contract.

In most situations, you will find that you are in a normal contract. In these cases, go for the extra tricks whenever the odds are in your favor - and, do so consistently.

— — — — — —

Most of the time you play a small percentage of the hands during any one session (unless you are a hand hog). Far more often you are challenged as a defender - where there are enormous pressures in matchpoints to restrict overtricks. For those who have not developed a good system with their partners, defense is largely a "hit or miss affair." In the next chapter we will present a comprehensive way of approaching this most difficult part of bridge.

QUIZ FOR CHAPTER 3

The answers to these problems begin on page 48. Get most of them right and your partner will let you play more hands!

1. | Contract: 4S
    | Lead: ♦A

♠92
♥Q65
♦954
♣K10863

♠AKQ103
♥A94
♦76
♣AQJ

West	North	East	South
	Pass	Pass	2NT
Pass	3♣[1]	Pass	3♠
Pass	3NT	Pass	4♠
(All pass)			

[1]Puppet Stayman, asking for a 5-card major

West starts with three top diamonds and you ruff the third. What is your plan?

2.

| Contract: 6S |
| Lead: ♣J |

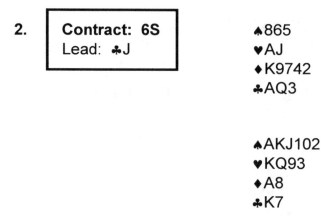

♠865
♥AJ
♦K9742
♣AQ3

♠AKJ102
♥KQ93
♦A8
♣K7

Bill Root's book, <u>How to Play a Bridge Hand</u>, contains a number of fine examples on how to vary your matchpoint play with the assessment of your contract. Here's one of them. The dummy goes down and you see that the combined hands are overpowered for 6S and you belong in 6NT - where most of the field will be. As South, how do you play this hand?

3.

| Contract: 4H |
| Lead: ♣2 |

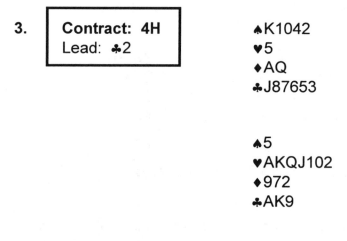

♠K1042
♥5
♦AQ
♣J87653

♠5
♥AKQJ102
♦972
♣AK9

West	North	East	South
			1♥
Pass	1NT	Pass	4♥
(All pass)			

On the ♣2, you play low from dummy, East ruffs and returns a trump. How do you play the hand?

4.

Contract: 3H
Lead: ♠K
Vul: Both

♠72
♥9852
♦AJ64
♣963

♠Q3
♥AKQ74
♦K102
♣J85

West	North	East	South
		Pass	1♥
1♠	2♥	2♠	Pass
Pass	3♥	(All pass)	

The defenders take their two spade tricks and switch to a trump. How do you play the hand?

5.

Contract: 1NT
Lead: ♦Q

♠AJ
♥J532
♦764
♣9853

♠K83
♥AK764
♦A9
♣Q62

This hand, taken from Root's book <u>How to Play a Bridge Hand</u>, illustrates another situation you will be faced with in a matchpoint contest. As South, you decided to open 1NT. After taking the opening diamond lead, how do you play the hand?

1.

| Contract: 4S |
| Lead: ♦A |

North
♠92
♥Q65
♦954
♣K10863

West
♠J854
♥KJ10
♦AKQJ2
♣2

East
♠76
♥8732
♦1083
♣9754

South
♠AKQ103
♥A94
♦76
♣AQJ

West	North	East	South
	Pass	Pass	2NT
Pass	3♣ [1]	Pass	3♠
Pass	3NT	Pass	4♠
(All pass)			

[1]Puppet Stayman, asking for a 5-card major

West starts with three top diamonds and you ruff the third. What is your plan?

Much of the field will be in 3NT, either going down or making just 9 tricks whenever the diamonds are breaking 4-4. So, you are in a great contract despite your 5-2 spade fit. The only danger is that you will lose control if the trumps break 4-2, as expected. You must safeguard your contract, even if it costs a trick. Give the opponents the ♠J immediately (lead the 10 from your hand). Then ruff the next diamond with dummy's ♠9 and claim the contract.

2.

Contract: 6S
Lead: ♣J

North
♠865
♥AJ
♦K9742
♣AQ3

West
♠Q4
♥8764
♦653
♣J1092

East
♠973
♥1052
♦QJ10
♣8654

South
♠AKJ102
♥KQ93
♦A8
♣K7

Bill Root's book, <u>How to Play a Bridge Hand</u>, contains a number of fine examples on how to vary your matchpoint play with the assessment of your contract. Here's one of them. The dummy goes down and you see that the combined hands are overpowered for 6S and you belong in 6NT - where most of the field will be. As South, how do you play this hand?

If the spade finesse is on, the field will make 13 tricks in 6NT and you will get a near bottom score. Your only hope is to play for the ♠Q to be offside (doubleton) - an anti-percentage play. If you fail, not much is lost - you had a bad board already. If you succeed you will make 7S and the field (losing the finesse) will make 6NT. You will edge the field by 20 points and get a top!

3.

Contract: 4H
Lead: ♣2

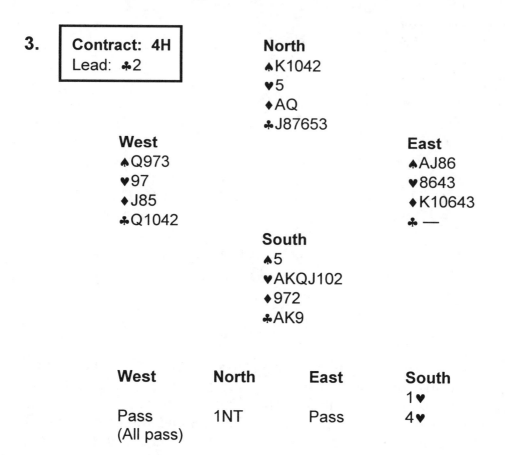

North
♠K1042
♥5
♦AQ
♣J87653

West
♠Q973
♥97
♦J85
♣Q1042

East
♠AJ86
♥8643
♦K10643
♣ —

South
♠5
♥AKQJ102
♦972
♣AK9

West	North	East	South
			1♥
Pass	1NT	Pass	4♥
(All pass)			

On the ♣2, you play low from dummy, East ruffs and returns a trump. How do you play the hand?

Had West opened a diamond, you would have had four potential losers: a spade, 2 diamonds and a club. By virtue of the club lead (1) you discover the bad break in that suit, (2) avoid the need to take the diamond finesse and (3) retain your diamond entry to the club suit. So, take advantage of this opening lead, by unblocking your ♣A on the first trick. Then take trumps out, play the ♣K and concede a club while the ♦A entry is still in dummy.

4.

Contract: 3H
Lead: ♠K
Vul: Both

North
♠72
♥9852
♦AJ64
♣963

West
♠AK1065
♥10
♦Q973
♣K104

East
♠J984
♥J63
♦85
♣AQ72

South
♠Q3
♥AKQ74
♦K102
♣J85

West	North	East	South
		Pass	1♥
1♠	2♥	2♠	Pass
Pass	3♥	(All pass)	

The defenders take their two spade tricks and switch to a trump. How do you play the hand?

The first thing you observe is that the opponents may be able to make three or perhaps even four spades. So, you could be in an *ideal* contract. This means you must hold your losses to down one because minus 200 would be a disaster. Therefore, you cannot afford to risk a diamond finesse and throw off a club loser if it wins. After taking out trumps, lead clubs - eventually the opponents will have to lead diamonds or give you a ruff and sluff. The idea is to play contracts safely when you think you are in a superior contract.

5.

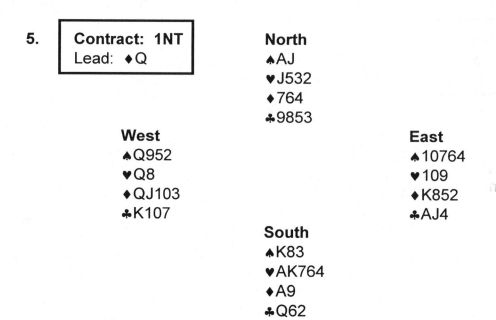

Contract: 1NT
Lead: ♦Q

North
♠AJ
♥J532
♦764
♣9853

West
♠Q952
♥Q8
♦QJ103
♣K107

East
♠10764
♥109
♦K852
♣AJ4

South
♠K83
♥AK764
♦A9
♣Q62

This hand, taken from Root's book <u>How to Play a Bridge Hand</u>, illustrates another situation you will be faced with in a matchpoint contest. As South, you decided to open 1NT. After taking the opening diamond lead, how do you play the hand?

A substantial part of the field will be in hearts, making one more trick than your contract. After testing the heart suit you find that the field will be scoring 140 as compared to your 120 in notrump. Your only chance for a good score is to take the spade finesse. If it works, you have nine tricks for a top score of 150. If it fails, don't worry; you were headed for a bad score anyway.

Chapter 4

THE FIVE LINES OF DEFENSE AND HOW TO USE THEM

Defense presents the greatest opportunity for you to gain a significant edge on the field and be a consistent winner in matchpoint events. More time at the table is spent on defense than on any of the other aspects of the game. It is by far the most difficult part of bridge. Declarer can see all 26 of his side's cards and is in sole command of the line of play, while defenders have neither of these advantages. They are totally dependent on **working out** what partner and declarer have in the way of values and shape and on **cooperation** from partner in the line of defense.

Being on defense is even more difficult in matchpoints. Setting the contract is sometimes not enough; in matchpoints you must restrict declarer to as few tricks as possible. Therefore, the pressure on defenders is **unrelenting** throughout each hand.

Typically, defense does not get the attention it deserves in spite of the edge that could be gained if partnerships devoted more effort to it. They discuss their system for bidding at great length but spend little or no time on a **system for defense**. Defenders are simply guessing much of the time. You will not have this problem if you and your partner carefully study the roadmap for defense in Figure 4-1 and follow it regularly.

The Overall System of Defense

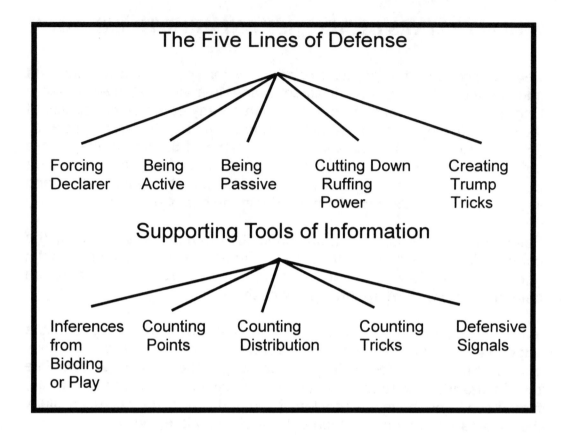

Figure 4-1

There are **five primary lines of defense**. They are the recurring themes that transcend every hand. We will take you through each one and show you how the expert chooses which defense to employ. Supporting these lines of defense are several **informational tools** that can be put to work for you as the hand unfolds. They will help you choose the correct line of defense.

1 - FORCE DECLARER TO LOSE CONTROL

The most powerful line of defense is the **force**. It causes declarer to lose control of the hand and to abandon side-suit winners (you may even completely take over the hand). The goal is to get control of declarer's own trump suit. The **force** is an ideal defense in matchpoints because it maximizes your potential for defensive tricks. Therefore, the **force**, when the right conditions are present, has priority over any other line of defense.

Conditions for Forcing Declarer

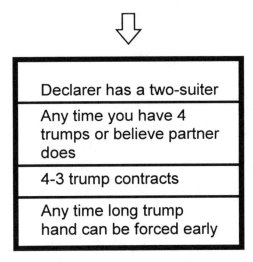

Declarer has a two-suiter
Any time you have 4 trumps or believe partner does
4-3 trump contracts
Any time long trump hand can be forced early

Figure 4-2

Figure 4-2 shows the various conditions that permit the forcing game to work. The purpose of the forcing game is to make it impossible for declarer to draw trumps and safely cash his side-suit tricks. This is particularly applicable to a two-suited hand where the forcing defense is easy to apply and achieves maximum results. It is easy to apply because declarer usually does not have longer than a five-card trump suit. Maximum results are achieved because the winners in the rest of declarer's hand (the second suit) can't be cashed if declarer loses control. Almost equally vulnerable to the force are contracts in which declarer is playing in a 4-3 trump fit or a 4-4 trump fit that breaks badly (4-1).

When one or more of the conditions in Figure 4-2 exist, the expert leads the partnership's most powerful suit. If it means leading from tenaces (such as AQ10, KJ10, AJ10) this is still the proper lead. Experts take the risk because it often pays off and the rewards are great. To illustrate:

Illustration Number 1

Contract: 4S
Lead: ♣3

North
♠J83
♥QJ7
♦KQ5
♣9752

West
♠7642
♥85
♦A3
♣KJ1063

East
♠9
♥K109643
♦8742
♣A8

South
♠AKQ105
♥A2
♦J1096
♣Q4

The expert leads a small club. Partner plays the ace and declarer follows with a small club. Partner returns the ♣8, declarer plays the queen and you take the king. You continue the ♣J, partner pitching off, and declarer ruffs. Declarer then uses all his trumps to draw yours, hoping your partner has the ♦A. When you get in with the ♦A, you cash your two good clubs to set the contract. These forcing plays sometimes defeat contracts and at other times just gain an extra trick or two for the defense. Either way, you are headed for a near top.

Illustration Number 2

| Contract: 4H |
| Lead: ♦A |

North
♠KQ84
♥Q1072
♦83
♣K95

West
♠92
♥A653
♦AKQ109
♣64

West	North	East	South
	Pass	Pass	1♥
2♦	3♦	Pass	4♥
(All pass)			

This is a relatively easy hand because you have four trumps and a strong suit to force declarer with. Declarer ruffs your third diamond in the dummy (with both partner and declarer following suit). Declarer attempts to take out trumps and partner follows to the first round. As long as you postpone taking your trump ace until the third round, the declarer is at your mercy. If he plays the third round, you take your ace and immediately force out the last trump in his hand. At this point you have control of the hand. If declarer does not lead the third round, he must concede a ruffing trick to you later on. Either way you have an excellent board.

Note that the very same kind of forcing defense can be accomplished when the opening leader is short and his partner is long in trumps. The opening leader forces declarer which promotes a trick in partner's hand or allows partner to take control of the hand. This is true partnership defense. The forcing game is the most effective weapon in the defensive arsenal and is fun to execute. (You might even get perverse pleasure out of watching declarer squirm when he realizes he is at your mercy!)

2 - GO ACTIVE WHEN TRICKS CAN DISAPPEAR

To do well at matchpoints, you must take all the tricks that belong to you - irrespective of whether the contract can be defeated. On many hands, if declarer is given enough time he will set up winners to pitch his losers on. Experts become very *active* whenever they think declarer is going to dispose of losers. Figure 4-3 illustrates the conditions for going *active*.

Conditions for Going Active

| Any time tricks can go away |
| Declarer's side suit is breaking |
| Vigorous bidding (slam interest) |
| Long running suits (e.g. Gambling 3NT) |

Figure 4-3

The important thing to remember about *active* defense is that usually you have everything to gain and nothing to lose. In other words, you can take high or even absurd risks because any tricks you might have had were going to go away anyway. The next two examples illustrate this concept.

Illustration Number 1

Contract: 4H
Lead: ?

West
♠A742
♥94
♦KJ42
♣1065

West	North	East	South
			1♥
Pass	2♣	Pass	2♥
Pass	3♥	Pass	4♥
(All pass)			

On this hand the expert, sitting West, will attack with his best suit (diamonds) because the bidding shows a good suit in the dummy, against which he has no defense. Any time you can tell from your own hand that the dummy's suit is going to break favorably, you know that a ready source of tricks is available to declarer. As soon as declarer gets into the lead, he will draw trumps and throw losers off on the side suit. In this case, if declarer had the ♦A and Q nothing would have been lost - your ♦K never would have taken a trick anyway. The full hand:

North
♠Q103
♥K8
♦1083
♣AKJ83

West
♠A742
♥94
♦KJ42
♣1065

East
♠J965
♥1065
♦A97
♣942

South
♠K8
♥AQJ742
♦Q65
♣Q7

Illustration Number 2

You sit East in the next hand and your partner leads a heart.

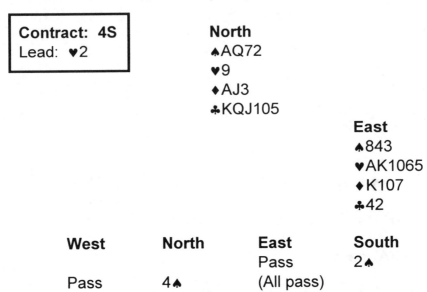

	Contract: 4S		**North**
Lead: ♥2		♠AQ72
		♥9
		♦AJ3
		♣KQJ105

North
♠AQ72
♥9
♦AJ3
♣KQJ105

East
♠843
♥AK1065
♦K107
♣42

West	**North**	**East**	**South**
		Pass	2♠
Pass	4♠	(All pass)	

You take the trick with the king. What is your next play?

The expert unhesitatingly will lead the ♦7. If declarer turns up with the ♦Q, nothing has been lost - his diamond losers would have disappeared on the club suit anyway. If partner has the ♣A, it will be too late then to dislodge the ♦A. Declarer will rise with the ♦A, draw trumps and run his clubs. Your only chance to get an extra trick on defense is to find partner with the ♦Q and the ♣A.

Often, defenders will have enough time to develop their tricks if they attack early enough. But, in some situations, it is "cash out" time at trick one. Typically, this is when declarer has shown a long running minor (such as with the Gambling 3NT bid) or when the bidding has been vigorous, showing slam interest. Here, defenders are wise to take whatever tricks they have right away.

Once you get into the habit of analyzing the bidding and your own hand (plus the dummy when it comes down), you can nearly always tell when your tricks are going away. As soon as you visualize that possibility, it is time to get going and develop your tricks or cash out. Although *active* defense is risky at times, you will be pleased with the outcome on most hands, and your matchpoint scores will go up.

3 - REMAIN PASSIVE WHEN YOUR TRICKS ARE SAFE

There are a number of other conditions (see Figure 4-4) which dictate just the opposite approach, that is, remaining *passive*. When such conditions exist, the main idea is to relax and not snatch winners, break suits for declarer or otherwise take him off the guess. The defender instead just sits back and waits for his tricks. When defenders are on lead (and they would rather not be), they must choose worthless suits, or top from sequences, or some other suit that will not give declarer anything. If experts initially are unsure about what to do, they will resist the temptation to go active. They would rather not risk doing the declarer's work for him.

Conditions for Remaining Passive

No evidence of strong side suit for declarer
Declarer very strong, dummy weak
A misfit or bad split in key suits
No real suit to lead against notrump
Defending 6NT and grand slams

Figure 4-4

The basic situation for electing to go *passive* is the *absence of any outside source of tricks* on which declarer can throw off his losers. Usually, the defender can tell from the bidding and a view of his cards and the dummy that (1) no side suit exists, or (2) if one exists it is breaking badly or (3) there is no entry to use the side suit. Experts are *passive* also when the *dummy is flat and weak* with little help for declarer. The expert will simply return declarer's leads or otherwise endplay him at every opportunity. Similarly, on *misfits* experts will make the most innocuous lead possible or remove what little ruffing power there is in the dummy.

Against notrump contracts, ragged 4-card suits usually are not useful for attack with the possible exception of an unbid major. Experts, instead, will try to find partner's suit or make a passive lead.

> "Against notrumps ... be very reluctant to lead from a 4-card suit with only one honor. Even with two honors 4-card suits present significant risks without great counter-balancing gain."   - Ron Klinger

Passive leads not only restrict overtricks; they can defeat contracts. Here are a couple of illustrations from Ron Klinger's book <u>50 Winning Duplicate Tips</u>.

Illustration No. 1

Contract: 3NT
Lead: ?

North
♠QJ4
♥875
♦K543
♣K103

West
♠A6
♥Q943
♦J876
♣854

East
♠K873
♥1062
♦92
♣AJ97

South
♠10952
♥AKJ
♦AQ10
♣Q62

West	North	East	South
Pass	Pass	Pass	1NT
Pass	2NT	Pass	3NT
(All pass)			

On this hand, you have no suit of your own, and so take a *passive* approach by leading the ♣8. Attacking from any of the other 3 suits gives declarer a gift and the contract. Once in a while these safe leads luckily hit partner, as in this case. Now, the declarer is limited to 8 tricks, and you've got your partner thinking you're a genius!

Illustration No. 2

```
┌─────────────────────┐
│ Contract:  1NT      │
│ Lead:  ?            │
└─────────────────────┘
```

North
♠ K754
♥ K7
♦ 9642
♣ J84

West
♠ Q98
♥ Q98
♦ 875
♣ KQ95

East
♠ J632
♥ 106432
♦ AK
♣ 73

South
♠ A10
♥ AJ5
♦ QJ103
♣ A1062

Leading the ♣K or the ♣5 allows declarer one or two extra tricks. The passive ♦8 on the other hand gives nothing away.

In **small slams** (played in notrump) and any **grand slam**, the declarer often needs to locate a missing honor. Here, experts lead suits that are least likely to give declarer an **unearned** trick.

Lawrence, in his new book on opening leads, notes still another test of whether you should take a passive approach. If the opponents bid strongly, they are likely to have their tricks, especially if you give them time. If the opponents staggered into game you should be more passive because there is a good chance they don't have enough tricks unless you give them some on the defense.

4 - CUT DOWN DECLARER'S RUFFING POWER

Knowing when to cut down the declarer's ruffing power is a sure way of reducing his tricks and getting a good matchpoint score. There are several conditions which should automatically trigger a trump lead. When these conditions arise you must lead trumps no matter how much it hurts. An expert will, for example, lead a trump from queen third when he knows it is right. He realizes that, at worst, the loss of a potential trump trick will be an even exchange but more often he will **gain** tricks.

Conditions for Cutting Down Declarer's Ruffing Power

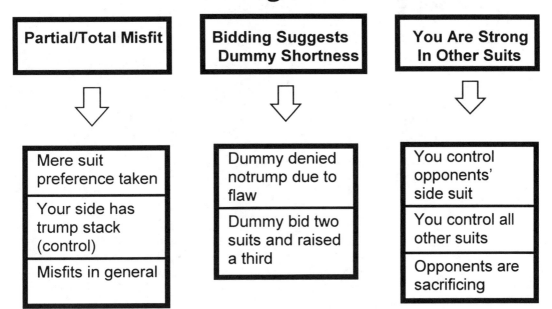

Partial/Total Misfit	Bidding Suggests Dummy Shortness	You Are Strong In Other Suits
Mere suit preference taken	Dummy denied notrump due to flaw	You control opponents' side suit
Your side has trump stack (control)	Dummy bid two suits and raised a third	You control all other suits
Misfits in general		Opponents are sacrificing

Figure 4-5

Notice that missing from the conditions above is the old adage "When in doubt lead trumps." This theory was disproved many years ago. To the contrary there should be a specific reason for leading trumps and there should be no doubt about it.

Partial or Total Misfits

Any partial or total misfit is a prime candidate for leading trumps. Misfits that come up most often are mere preferences taken by declarer's partner in a partscore contract. For example, in the auction below partner has left declarer in his second suit - a minor - and neither defender was able to balance (clearly a misfit situation). It is certain that dummy's spades, declarer's first bid suit, will be extremely short and dummy's diamonds may not be much longer. Declarer will be anxious to ruff out his spade losers - he will not be happy to see a trump lead on the table.

To illustrate:

```
┌─────────────────────┐
│ Contract:  2D       │
│ Lead:  ♦3           │
└─────────────────────┘
```

North
♠6
♥Q9743
♦Q76
♣K1064

West
♠K32
♥A1082
♦A93
♣875

East
♠Q1095
♥J6
♦852
♣AQ93

South
♠AJ874
♥K5
♦KJ104
♣J2

West	North	East	South
			1♠
Pass	1NT	Pass	2♦
(All pass)			

Other than a spade, heart and 3 diamonds, the declarer will have to scrounge for tricks. Ruffing out losers is his best chance of getting eight tricks. The only way to prevent this is to lead a small trump or the ace followed by a small trump. The very best that declarer can do now is ruff out one spade loser. After successive trump leads, declarer will be in a hopeless situation, with nothing but losers in the dummy and in his own hand - down two.

Trump leads are desirable also when mere suit preference is taken during auctions which reveal a two-suited or three-suited hand. You can tell because the opponents usually will use conventional bids such as Michaels, Unusual Notrump, Flannery and Roman to convey their distribution . Those bids combined with a preference auction practically scream for a trump lead before declarer starts the ruffing process.*

In all preference or misfit auctions, the declarer will try to trump out his side suit losers and, if he is lucky, any overruffing by a defender will be done with a natural trump trick (loser on loser). So, it is up to the defenders to neutralize the declarer's strategy and lead trumps.

Your Side Has a Trump Stack

There are distinct advantages to taking ownership of the trump suit whenever you have a strong holding, and the way to do this is to simply lead trumps. Once you own the trump suit you are now the declarer and control the hand. It is important to lead trumps early before the declarer can ruff losers in the dummy or take ruffing tricks with *small* trumps in his own hand. Leading trumps, as opposed to other suits, on these types of hands can make a great difference in the final result - as many as 4 or 5 tricks.

The usual conditions for leading trumps at the very outset are when your partner converts your one-level take-out double to penalty (by passing) or when one of you risks a two-level double of the opponents' suit because a lot of your values are in that suit. Illustrations of trump holdings for these kinds of doubles are:

One-level Penalty	Two-level Penalty
KJ1098	KQJ9

---

*Some of these conventional bids are two-suited ones. Elsewhere, we urge a forcing game on two-suited hands. But the forcing game presumes a *fit* auction. Here we are talking about *preference (misfit)* auctions.

A good example of the proper lead for two-level penalty doubles comes from a new book on opening leads by Mike Lawrence (see Chapter 10).

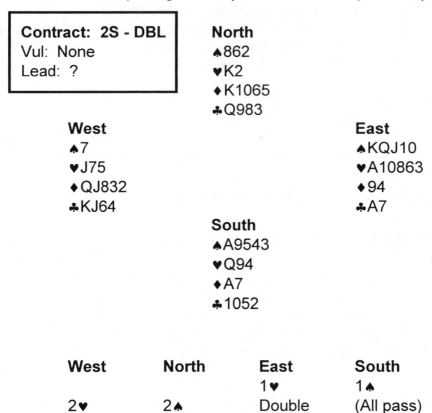

Contract: 2S - DBL			
Vul: None			
Lead: ?			

North
♠862
♥K2
♦K1065
♣Q983

West
♠7
♥J75
♦QJ832
♣KJ64

East
♠KQJ10
♥A10863
♦94
♣A7

South
♠A9543
♥Q94
♦A7
♣1052

West	North	East	South
		1♥	1♠
2♥	2♠	Double	(All pass)

Note that West, with only a 3-card raise, trusted his partner and sat for the double. If West further cooperates and leads a trump, East will be able to remove dummy's trumps and score a two-trick set, an excellent result.

Your Hand - Opponents Are Sacrificing

Whenever you as defenders have control over all three of the other suits or the opponents are sacrificing, the best thing to do is to immediately reduce declarer's ruffing power. You must do so to protect your own tricks; otherwise, some of them will be ruffed out. When opponents sacrifice, laying down a trump on opening lead is almost automatic.

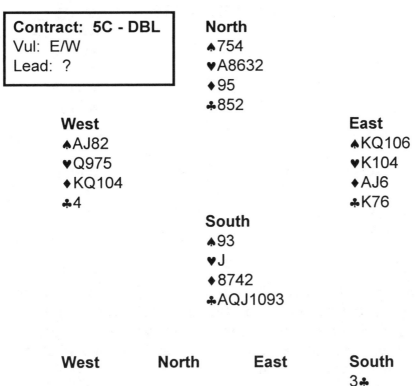

Contract: 5C - DBL
Vul: E/W
Lead: ?

North
♠754
♥A8632
♦95
♣852

West
♠AJ82
♥Q975
♦KQ104
♣4

East
♠KQ106
♥K104
♦AJ6
♣K76

South
♠93
♥J
♦8742
♣AQJ1093

West	North	East	South
			3♣
Double	5♣	Double	(All pass)

If West starts with the ♣4 (not the ♦K), East will get in twice to continue trump leads. South will then lose 4 diamonds and 2 spades for down 4. If trumps are not led right away, South will go down 3 which is less than East/West's vulnerable game.

Trump Leads Are Not Always Easy to Predict

In time, you will become familiar with the conditions that dictate trump leads. However, trump opening leads are not always predictable. In those cases, defenders can recover after the opening lead and still do serious damage. For example, when the shortness appears as the dummy goes down and there is no source of tricks to dispose of declarer's losers - a trump lead is the obvious switch. To illustrate:

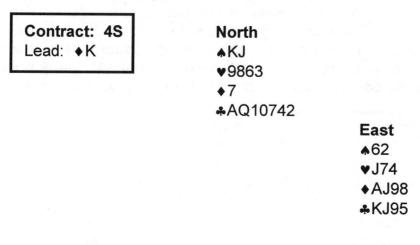

	Contract: 4S		North
	Lead: ♦K		♠KJ
			♥9863
			♦7
			♣AQ10742

East
♠62
♥J74
♦AJ98
♣KJ95

West	North	East	South
			1♠
Pass	2♣	Pass	3♠
Pass	4♠	(All pass)	

Your partner opens the ♦K. What do you do? The club suit is no threat because you have it all locked up. But, declarer obviously has diamond losers to worry about. Therefore, the expert will overtake partner's ♦K and lead trumps. He will take control because he knows what to do and partner is unaware of the club situation.

5 - CREATING TRUMP TRICKS

Both ruffing out declarer's tricks and promoting trump tricks of your own are excellent ways to develop defensive tricks (see Figure 4-6).

Conditions for Creating Trump Tricks

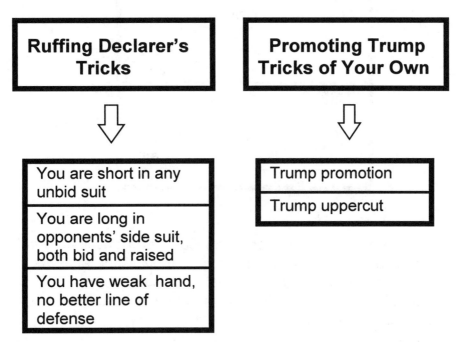

Figure 4-6

The practice of leading short suits and ruffing out declarer's tricks is the most widely practiced line of defense in bridge and needs no further explanation here, except to say that the practice is abused. Too often your short suit is declarer's long side suit. Unless you use this line of defense discretely, you will give the declarer both timing in the play of the hand and assistance in developing his side suit. Experts tend to go for ruffs under three conditions:

- When they have no natural trump tricks of their own.
- When they can reasonably expect an entry to bring off the ruff (possession of a high trump honor, for example).
- When the situation is desperate and there is no better line of defense.

Used less, but a more effective weapon, is the magic of creating trump tricks where none exist! This practice involves the trump promotion play and the uppercut.

In a **trump promotion** play, declarer is placed in a position where he must ruff high and, in so doing, promote a trump trick for the defenders.

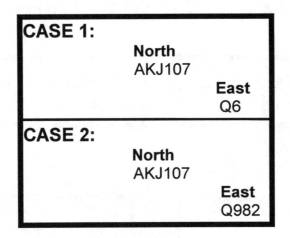

In case 1, any lead which both North and East can ruff will automatically promote East's queen into a trick. In case 2, if the East defender is patient and refuses to overruff the jack or ten, a second trump trick will be created. Sometimes, even just forcing the dummy to ruff will promote a trump trick, as shown below.

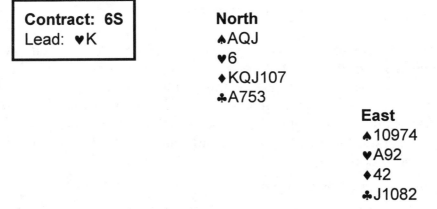

The declarer is in 6 spades and your partner opens the ♥K. Taking no chances, the expert will overtake the king with the ace and lead a heart back. This guarantees (promotes) a trump trick in his hand to defeat the contract.

Another popular way among the experts to create a trump trick is by way of an *uppercut*. Here, a defender ruffs in with his highest trump to weaken declarer's holding, in the hope that it will create a trump trick for partner.

For example:

Contract: 4S	
Lead: ♦A	

North
♠AQ7
♥Q9
♦Q5
♣KJ5432

West
♠J108
♥103
♦A86
♣AQ876

East
♠95
♥7642
♦KJ10974
♣10

South
♠K6432
♥AKJ85
♦32
♣9

West	North	East	South
			1♠
Pass	2♣	3♦	3♥
Pass	3♠	Pass	4♠
(All pass)			

West leads the ♦A - the suit his partner bid during the auction. East encourages and after taking the king, lays down his ♣10. His partner rises with the ace and leads a low one back, aware that both partner and declarer can ruff. Partner cooperates by ruffing with his highest spade (the 9) and a trump trick is created for partner out of thin air - like magic!

When you have exhausted all means of collecting defensive tricks, be careful not to overlook a trump promotion or uppercut. They are wonderful ways to create an extra trick for you and a great result on the hand.

INFORMATION TOOLS SUPPORTING THE FIVE LINES OF DEFENSE

Your overall system of defense consists of the *five primary lines of defense* just discussed and several tools of information that can be put to work for you whenever you like. Instead of stumbling around on defense, the information provided by these tools will either tip you off to the correct *line of defense* or keep you on track. Let's see what these tools are:

Information Tools Supporting the Five Lines of Defense

Inferences from ⇩	Counting ⇩	Clear Signals ⇩
• Bidding • Partner's leads and signals • Declarer's line of play	• Tricks • Shape • Points	• Attitude • Count • Suit preference

Figure 4-7

Inferences from the Bidding and Play

The bidding process itself provides a rough idea of possible leads, location of any strong suits, who's got what values and approximately what the shape is around the table. Other inferences that build up a picture of the unseen hands are partner's leads and signals, as well as declarer's early line of play.*

---

*An entire book could be written on the subject of *inferences* and, in fact, one has (see <u>Dormer on Deduction</u>). In our book, inferences are discussed not in one place but instead throughout each chapter.

Counting Shape

The initial impressions formed from inferences are further refined by counting actual shape, points and tricks as the hand proceeds. While the expert is counting, he keeps asking the question "What is declarer up to?" or "What's going on?" This is how experts time after time pull off their sensational victories.

> **"The player who takes the trouble to work out the enemy holdings will always enjoy an advantage over the mechanical player who sees only the cards in front of his nose. Counting the hand may seem a laborious chore to begin with but it quickly becomes second nature, and it brings big rewards on those occasions when it turns a guess into a certainty. Problems in play and defense tend to melt away like snow on a summer's day when you make an effort to count. Quite simply, counting makes the difference between winning and losing."**
> **- Hugh Kelsey**

Experts will sometimes claim their defensive tricks ahead of time or even claim the declarer's hand for him! This is quite impressive until you learn how easy counting is.

Counting seems like hard work. However, after several months of practice it becomes second nature. Also, counting the hands can be simplified if you follow the concept - knowing the shape of 3 hands makes the 4th a given. The suits in your hand and dummy obviously are visible to you. If you can reconstruct just one suit in either of the two unseen hands, then the distribution of that suit is known around the table. And, when you know the shape of 3 suits in either partner's or declarer's hand, then, of course, you know the 4th. It follows then, that when you know the full shape of just one unseen hand, the remaining unseen hand becomes a given and distribution of all 52 cards is revealed.

The counting process starts with the particular unseen hand (declarer's or partner's) about which you have the most information. An illustration follows.

Distribution

	♠ ♥ ♦ ♣
Your hand:	**2 4 2 5**
Dummy:	**3 3 4 3**

Bidding

Declarer	Dummy
1♠	1NT
2♥	3♠
4♠	Pass

Training Your Mind to Count the Cards

ACTION	DECLARER'S DISTRIBUTION	PARTNER'S DISTRIBUTION
Inference from bidding	*5 4 2 2*	*? ? ? ?*
Early declarer play: • Ruffed 2nd club	*? ? ? 1*	*? ? ? 4*
• Took out trumps in two rounds, partner's queen fell	*6 ? ? 1*	*2 ? ? 4*
• Led hearts once, partner gave count	*6 4 ? 1*	*2 2 ? 4*
Full hand after five cards played	*6 4 2 1*	*2 2 5 4*

Figure 4-8

Because of better information, the process of counting is easier on some hands than on others. However, an approximate count is still much better than none; it can save you from making a stupid error. The usual reasons for failing to count are laziness and overconfidence. This won't happen to you if you stay focused on each hand and use the simple counting process discussed above.

Counting Points

Somewhat the same approach is used in constructing hand values (points). First, bidding inferences provide approximate point count around the table. Then, from looking at the two visible hands and early play of the cards, experts can surmise the actual location or absence of specific honor cards.

Here is a situation where pinpointing honor cards and just a partial count on the hand saved the day.

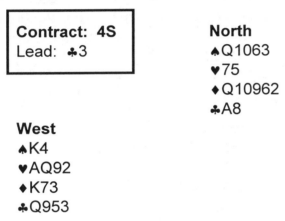

Contract: 4S	**North**
Lead: ♣3	♠Q1063
	♥75
	♦Q10962
	♣A8

West
♠K4
♥AQ92
♦K73
♣Q953

West	North	East	South
			1♠
Double	2NT[1]	3♣	4♠
(All pass)			

[1]Limit raise or better

On the club lead declarer rose with the ace and lost the trump finesse to West's king. Declarer ruffed the club continuation, took another round of trumps (partner following), and played a small diamond from his hand. How do you defend?

You figure it out. Based on the bidding, is declarer marked with the ♦A?

You	14
Dummy	8
Pard	4*
Declarer	<u>??</u>
Total	40

*♣K and J

Declarer is known also to have 5 spades, 1 club and therefore 7 cards in the red suits. Five of these will be taken care of by the diamonds in dummy, so his two heart losers will remain. Since your two heart tricks will not disappear, step up with the ♦K and return a *passive* diamond. Otherwise, declarer will play the ♦Q, then the ace and he will endplay you with a third diamond! Note how information on both points and shape supported your decision on your line of defense - whether to go active or passive. The full deal:

North
♠Q1063
♥75
♦Q10962
♣A8

West
♠K4
♥AQ92
♦K73
♣Q953

East
♠75
♥863
♦85
♣KJ10764

South
♠AJ982
♥KJ104
♦AJ4
♣2

Counting Tricks

Counting declarer's expected tricks as well as your own is necessary on some hands before choosing the proper line of defense. That knowledge will tell you (1) whether the contract can be set and, if so, how to proceed and (2) whether to cash out or just sit back and play a passive defense. The next hand can be set but only if you count both points around the table and declarer's tricks.

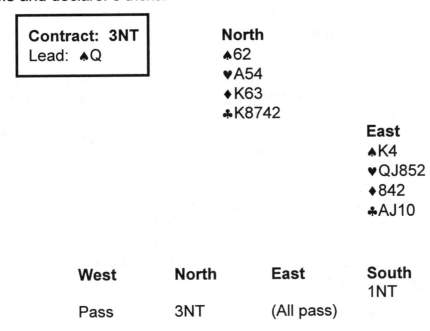

```
┌─────────────────────┐
│ Contract: 3NT       │
│ Lead: ♠Q            │
└─────────────────────┘
```

North
♠62
♥A54
♦K63
♣K8742

East
♠K4
♥QJ852
♦842
♣AJ10

West	North	East	South
			1NT
Pass	3NT	(All pass)	

You are sitting East and your partner opens the ♠Q. What is your plan?

Overtake the ♠Q and, if declarer allows you to hold the trick, as he must, switch to a small heart. Declarer and dummy have about 26 points and you have 11. That leaves partner with about 3 points - the ♠Q and J and no entry. Declarer has 7 or 8 tricks (1 spade, 2 hearts, 3 or 4 diamonds and 1club). Therefore, he will have to develop the club suit to make his contract. If partner has the ♥10, your two club entries will provide enough time to bring the hearts home and defeat the contract. If he doesn't, it won't matter. Declarer will still set up the club suit and you'll get the only three tricks you had coming - one spade and two clubs.

Clear and Unambiguous Partnership Signals

Defensive signals are a form of legal table talk. The best uses of defensive signals are to (1) *direct the line of defense* and (2) permit defenders to *operate as a partnership*. Other purposes are determining count, locating high cards, creating lines of communication and providing special information with leads. The problem is that there are a lot of signalling methods or variations on their use today, none of which satisfy all the needs and with no widespread consensus among the experts as to which is best. Some important observations are:

- Experimentation on signalling methods continues among the experts. For example, some experts are experimenting with giving up much of the count signal in favor of suit preference.* The universe of bridge hands is so large that it takes years to assess the value of this kind of change.

- Whatever signalling method you adopt, the most important signal is at trick one to confirm the initial line of defense or to ask for a switch to the proper one. The third-hand defender should take a few moments to think out the hand before playing to trick one. If a break in tempo is required, advise the declarer that you are thinking about the whole hand.

- You cannot create understandings on the spot. You must have good partnership understandings and then *stick to your system*. Nothing tends to split open a partnership more then a disorganized defense which allows declarer to bring home an unmakeable contract because the defenders were unable to communicate clearly with each other.

- Take control whenever you know what to do. Do not rely on your signalling system (no matter how good it is). Make defense as easy as possible for partner; he will appreciate it.

- There are different signalling methods which will accomplish the same purpose. Your system should include these essentials:

---

*See, for example, A Switch in Time, Pamela and Matthew Granovetter.

Essentials of Any Signalling Method

- An encouraging signal when partner has embarked on what seems to be the proper line of defense

- An encouraging signal when any switch would be a disaster

- A discouraging signal when a switch in the line of defense is needed:

  — The desired switch may be an obvious one such as dummy's weakness.

  — The desired switch may require the opening leader to further work out the hand now that the dummy has been revealed. Here, there is no substitute for common sense and knowledge of the five lines of defense. For example he might have to counter declarer's next move such as:

  - - Ruffing out losers in the dummy, or

  - - Using dummy's side suit winners to dispose of losers.

  — The desired switch may be so unlikely (such as dummy's strongest suit) that your partnership will need a special signal to handle these unusual cases.

Figure 4-9

- No matter what signalling method you adopt, there are no illusive shortcuts, crutches, or substitutes for working out *what's going on* and *what declarer is up to* as the hand progresses - including hand *distribution* and *high card location*.

Signalling Methods

Figure 4-10 displays the primary signalling methods. You will see that upside down attitude and count are used in the illustration. This is because an increasing number of experts, including those on the European continent, are using them on the grounds that they have an edge over standard signals. A good time to explore upside down signals is when your *regular* partners are willing to try the change.

Highlights of Expert Signalling Methods (Using Upside Down Count and Attitude)

SIGNAL ⇩	APPLICATION	PURPOSE	HOW SIGNALS OPERATE
ATTITUDE	Applies to suit partner has led	Directs the line of defense	• Low card suggests continue • High card urges switch
COUNT	Applies to suit declarer has led	Helps construct unseen hands	• High card = odd distribution • Low card = even distribution
SUIT PREFERENCE	Applies when attitude/count not applicable	Pinpoints suit for reentry or switch	• Two kinds: standard and unusual • 2nd card after count or attitude may be suit preference
DISCARDS	Applies when you can not follow suit	First card attitude, then present count	• On declarer's winners, discard 1st suit(s) you can't stop • Plan ahead, never discard in pain

Figure 4-10

Note that *attitude* directs the line of defense and does not necessarily show interest in the suit led. In fact, an encouraging card may reflect no interest in the suit - the logical switch may be worse.

To illustrate:

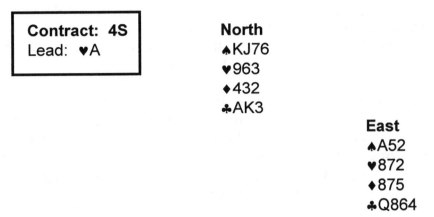

Contract: 4S	North
Lead: ♥A	♠KJ76
	♥963
	♦432
	♣AK3

East
♠A52
♥872
♦875
♣Q864

Partner leads the ♥A and, as East, what do you play?

The logical switch is diamonds but a switch to that suit could easily give up a trick. So, you encourage on the first heart and hope for the best. In this regard, a discouraging signal is actually stronger than an encouraging one in that it asks partner specifically to make a switch.

A switch can also be asked for by the person making the lead. He does this on opening lead or during the hand by leading a high spot card. For example:

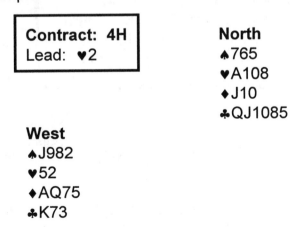

Contract: 4H	North
Lead: ♥2	♠765
	♥A108
	♦J10
	♣QJ1085

West
♠J982
♥52
♦AQ75
♣K73

Dummy's ♥8 wins the trump lead and declarer loses a club finesse to West's king. The club suit is now a real threat to dispose of declarer's remaining losers and both defenders can see the danger. A low spade would ask for return of that suit. The expert instead would select a high spade spot to show no interest. If partner has the ace, he will automatically return dummy's weakness, a diamond, and defeat the contract.

Giving **count** when the declarer leads a suit depends on two things. Is it safe to reveal the information and does partner need the information? When in doubt, count is given. Experts will also give count when discarding a suit. The first discard is attitude and additional ones show how many cards remain in the same suit (present count).

Suit preference takes a back seat to attitude and count signals in many systems. If a signal could mean either attitude or count, it is not suit preference. Misuse of these signals (that is, using one when partner thinks it is another) is a source of much confusion and distrust in partnerships. Experts tend to live with their system - they do not improvise and create understandings on the spot and expect partner to "work it out."

Standard suit preference signals are those that come up often and tell which side suit (lower or higher ranking) partner should return. **Unusual** suit preference situations come up much more rarely. They consist of an abnormally low or high card to show interest in a lower or higher ranking suit. For example, if you make an unfortunate opening lead of an ace and the dummy comes down with the KQJ6 of that suit, an abnormally high or low card played by your partner **automatically** is suit preference.

> "On defense you should always try to imagine what your partner is thinking and what information he needs most. Then send him that information as clearly as possible."
> - Eric Kokish

Never Force Your Partner to Guess If You Know What to Do

As good as your signalling methods may be, we repeat, do not rely on them when you know what to do. In other words, don't assume that what is obvious to you will be obvious to your partner also. The rule is **never put partner on a guess if you can help it**.

To illustrate:

```
┌─────────────────────┐          North
│ Contract: 4S        │          ♠K43
│ Lead: ♣A            │          ♥97
└─────────────────────┘          ♦KJ10
                                 ♣Q8753
```

West
♠2
♥Q108642
♦A75
♣AK9

West	North	East	South
			1♠
2♥	2♠	Pass	4♠
(All pass)			

You lead the ♣A and partner signals that he holds a doubleton. If you continue with the ♣K and 9 to give him a ruff, he will likely return a heart (your bid suit, dummy's weakness and indicated suit preference). Declarer will then take his ♥A and pitch his diamond losers on dummy's clubs. So, in these kinds of situations you simply take control and cash your ♦A before giving partner his ruff. Your partner will thank you later.

- - - - - -

Now that you are well versed in the five lines of defense and the informational tools supporting their use, the next chapter prepares you to make the all-important killing lead. Because of the close relationship between these two chapters you will find some overlap. If you missed anything in this chapter, hopefully you will pick it up in the next. But, first a tough quiz.

QUIZ FOR CHAPTER 4

The answers to these problems begin on page 98. If you get about 12 of them correct, you are a good defender. If you get about 16 of them correct, people will be begging you to play with them. If you get all 21 correct, the experts will pay you to play with them!

1.

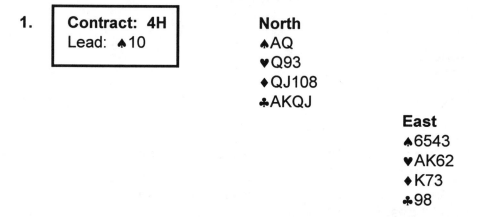

Contract: 4H	North
Lead: ♠10	♠AQ
	♥Q93
	♦QJ108
	♣AKQJ

East
♠6543
♥AK62
♦K73
♣98

Partner leads the ♠10 which is taken by the ace in dummy. Declarer leads a low heart, you duck and he takes it with the jack. On the next trump lead, partner discards an encouraging diamond and you take your ♥K. What is your next play?

2.

Contract: 4H
Lead: ?

West
♠5
♥9875
♦K9764
♣A93

West	North	East	South
			1♥
Pass	1NT	Pass	3♣
Pass	3♥	Pass	4♥
(All pass)			

Sitting West, what is your line of defense?

3.

Contract: 6H
Lead: ?

West
♠K74
♥54
♦109873
♣A62

West	North	East	South
	1♣	Pass	1♥
Pass	3♣	Pass	3♥
Pass	4♥	Pass	6♥
(All pass)			

Sitting West, what is your line of defense?

4.

Contract: 5H
Lead: ?

West
♠QJ10742
♥95
♦Q73
♣KQ

West	North	East	South
			1♥
1♠	2♣	3♠	4♥
Pass	Pass	4♠	Pass
Pass	5♥	(All pass)	

Sitting West, what is your line of defense?

5.

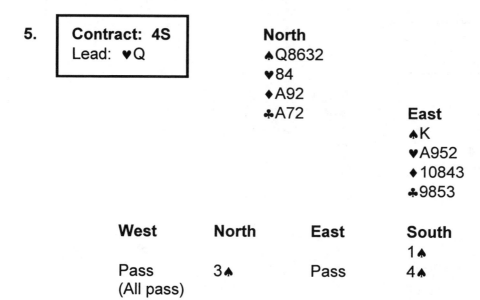

		Contract: 4S			Lead: ♥Q	

North
♠Q8632
♥84
♦A92
♣A72

East
♠K
♥A952
♦10843
♣9853

West	North	East	South
			1♠
Pass	3♠	Pass	4♠
(All pass)			

You take your partner's ♥Q with the ace. What is your line of defense?

6.

Contract: 1NT
Lead: ?

West
♠Q98
♥Q98
♦875
♣KQ95

West	North	East	South
	Pass	Pass	1NT
(All pass)			

What is your line of defense?

7.

┌─────────────────────┐
│ **Contract: 5C(DBL)** │
│ Lead: ?   │
└─────────────────────┘

West
♠Q109762
♥72
♦J96
♣K3

West	North	East	South
2♠	4NT[1]	Double	5♣
Pass	Pass	Double	(All pass)

[1]Shows minor suits

What is your line of defense?

8.

┌─────────────────┐
│ **Contract: 3H** │
│ Lead: ?   │
└─────────────────┘

West
♠K1086
♥K42
♦QJ106
♣J4

West	North	East	South
Pass	2♦[1]	Pass	2♥
Pass	Pass	3♣	3♥
(All pass)			

[1]Flannery (5 hearts, 4 spades)

What is your line of defense?

9.

Contract: 4H
Lead: ♣2

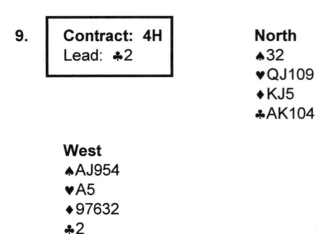

North
♠32
♥QJ109
♦KJ5
♣AK104

West
♠AJ954
♥A5
♦97632
♣2

West	North	East	South
			1♣
1♠	Double¹	Pass	2♥
Pass	4♥	(All pass)	

¹Negative

Declarer wins your club lead with dummy's ace; partner plays the 9 and declarer the 3. Declarer starts on trumps and you win the ace. What is your lead at trick three?

10.

Contract: 4S
Lead: ♥K

North
♠874
♥863
♦AQJ
♣AQJ8

East
♠A5
♥A4
♦98532
♣7653

Your partner opens a weak 2H bid and the opponents proceed to 4S. Partner leads the ♥K. What is your line of defense?

11.

Contract: 4S
Lead: ?

West
- ♠A7
- ♥J54
- ♦J1092
- ♣A863

West	North	East	South
	1♣	Pass	1♠
Pass	2♠	Pass	3♣
Pass	4♠	(All pass)	

What is your line of defense?

12.

Contract: 4H
Lead: ♠A

North
- ♠J104
- ♥AQ82
- ♦KQJ43
- ♣6

East
- ♠Q872
- ♥9765
- ♦5
- ♣9743

West	North	East	South
1♣	Double	Pass	2♣
3♣	3♦	4♣	4♥
(All pass)			

Your partner takes the ♠A and K and leads to your queen; everybody follows. What next?

13.

Contract: 4S
Lead: ♦A

North
♠J984
♥84
♦QJ109
♣A72

West
♠76
♥AJ6
♦AK2
♣109854

West	North	East	South
1♣	Pass	1♥	1♠
Double[1]	2♠	3♣	4♠
(All pass)			

[1]Support double (shows 3 hearts)

After opening the ♦A, you switch to the ♣10. Declarer rises with the ace and partner drops the king, showing a sequence. Declarer plays trumps twice; your partner shows out on the second trump trick. Declarer then tables a small diamond and you take your king. What next?

14.

Contract: 4S
Lead: ♥5

North
♠J10743
♥83
♦K952
♣Q7

East
♠965
♥A106
♦J84
♣KJ62

West	North	East	South
			1♠
Pass	2♠	Pass	3NT
Pass	4♠	(All pass)	

As East, you take the ♥A and return partner's lead. He wins the jack and switches to the ♣9. Dummy plays the ♣7, you the jack and declarer the ace. Declarer draws trumps in three rounds (partner shows out after one) and plays the ♥Q, partner covers with the K and the trick is ruffed in dummy. Declarer then leads the ♣Q from the dummy and drops the 10 on your king. What is your next play?

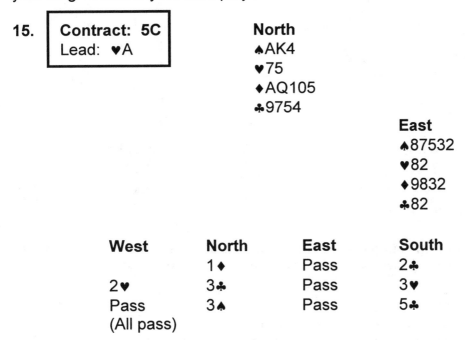

15.

| Contract: 5C |
| Lead: ♥A |

North
♠AK4
♥75
♦AQ105
♣9754

East
♠87532
♥82
♦9832
♣82

West	North	East	South
	1♦	Pass	2♣
2♥	3♣	Pass	3♥
Pass	3♠	Pass	5♣
Pass			
(All pass)			

After overcalling the suit, partner leads the ♥A (from AK). What do you do with your yarborough?

93

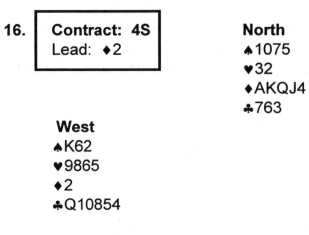

16. Contract: 4S
Lead: ♦2

North
♠1075
♥32
♦AKQJ4
♣763

West
♠K62
♥9865
♦2
♣Q10854

West	North	East	South
Pass	Pass	1♥	1♠
2♥	3♠	Pass	4♠
(All pass)			

You lead your stiff diamond, dummy wins, East plays the 3 and declarer the 5. Declarer finesses the trump king and you win. How should you continue?

17. Contract: 6NT
Lead: ♥10

North
♠KJ1065
♥AQJ6
♦—
♣6532

East
♠Q987
♥4
♦J963
♣9874

West	North	East	South
	1♠	Pass	3♦
Pass	3♥	Pass	4NT
Pass	5♦	Pass	6NT
(All pass)			

The declarer won your partner's heart lead with his king, laid down three top diamonds and then gave you your jack. Playing standard signals, partner followed three times with the ♦2, 8, and 7 and then discarded the

94

♥9. Declarer discarded three clubs and a spade from the dummy. It is your play.

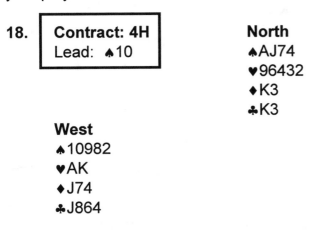

18.

Contract: 4H	
Lead: ♠10	

North
♠AJ74
♥96432
♦K3
♣K3

West
♠10982
♥AK
♦J74
♣J864

West	North	East	South
			1♥
Pass	3♥	Pass	4♥
(All pass)			

On your spade lead declarer plays the ace and your partner follows with the 3 (you are playing standard signals). Declarer plays a trump to your king; how do you continue?

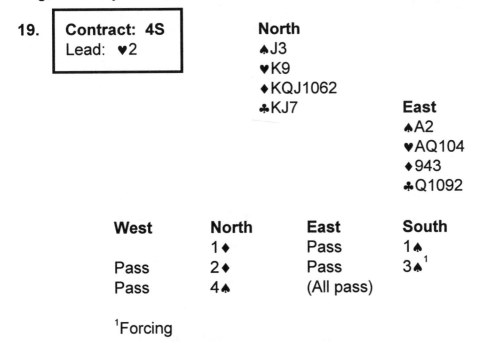

19.

Contract: 4S	
Lead: ♥2	

North
♠J3
♥K9
♦KQJ1062
♣KJ7

East
♠A2
♥AQ104
♦943
♣Q1092

West	North	East	South
	1♦	Pass	1♠
Pass	2♦	Pass	3♠[1]
Pass	4♠	(All pass)	

[1]Forcing

Your partner starts the attack with his fourth best heart, the two. You take the ♥Q and lead what?

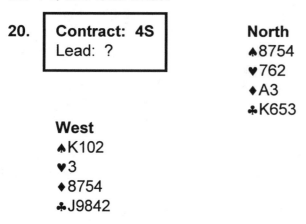

20. | **Contract: 4S**
Lead: ?

North
♠8754
♥762
♦A3
♣K653

West
♠K102
♥3
♦8754
♣J9842

West	North	East	South
			1♠
Pass	2♠	4♥	4♠
(All pass)			

This is one of those cases where the lead is obvious, the stiff ♥3 (your partner's suit). Partner takes the trick and leads two more rounds. But, declarer ruffs the third round with his ♠Q. Your play?

21. | **Contract: 3S**
Lead: ♦K

North
♠QJ10
♥542
♦A10
♣KQJ76

West
♠A942
♥K108
♦KQJ96
♣A

West	North	East	South
	1♣	Pass	1♠
Double	2♠	Pass	Pass
3♦	Pass	Pass	3♠
(All pass)			

Declarer takes your ♦K with dummy's ace and leads the ♠Q which you duck. He leads the ♠J, your partner pitches off a diamond, and you duck again. If declarer leads another spade you will take the ace, force

96

declarer with diamonds and eventually take control. But, declarer foils your efforts and leads the ♣K. Partner plays a low one (upside down signals) and you win your ace. You return a low heart and partner's queen goes to declarer's ace. Declarer finally leads the third round of trumps and you take your ace. Can you still defeat the contract? How?

1.

| Contract: 4H |
| Lead: ♠10 |

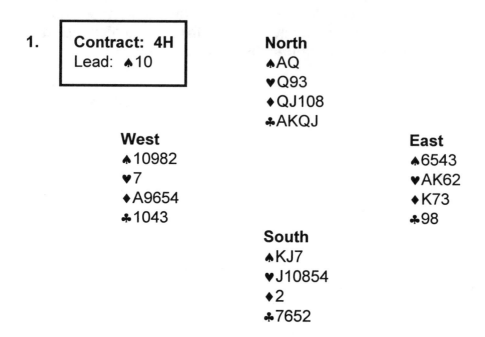

North
♠AQ
♥Q93
♦QJ108
♣AKQJ

West
♠10982
♥7
♦A9654
♣1043

East
♠6543
♥AK62
♦K73
♣98

South
♠KJ7
♥J10854
♦2
♣7652

Partner leads the ♠10 which is taken by the ace in dummy. Declarer leads a low trump, you duck and he wins with the jack. On the next trump lead, partner discards an encouraging diamond and you take your ♥K. What is your next play?

Play the ♦K. If declarer has two diamonds he goes down immediately. If he has only one declarer can be forced. When you get in with your second heart honor, force declarer again with another diamond. He must trump and promote a trump trick for you or give up a diamond trick. Notice that if you lead a low diamond first, declarer can not be forced because your king will be ruffed out on the next round.

LINE OF DEFENSE - FORCING DECLARER

2.

Contract: 4H
Lead: ?

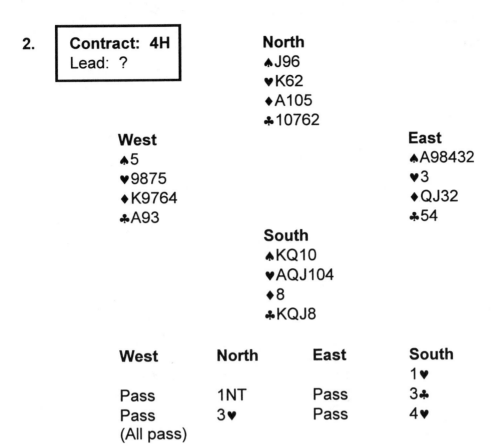

North
♠J96
♥K62
♦A105
♣10762

West
♠5
♥9875
♦K9764
♣A93

East
♠A98432
♥3
♦QJ32
♣54

South
♠KQ10
♥AQJ104
♦8
♣KQJ8

West	North	East	South
			1♥
Pass	1NT	Pass	3♣
Pass	3♥	Pass	4♥
(All pass)			

Sitting West, what is your line of defense?

Lead a small diamond. Whenever the declarer shows a two-suited hand, the best line of defense when you have four trumps is "the forcing game." Declarer will first take out trumps and give the defenders one of their two aces. Then, a diamond continuation removes declarer's last trump. He has at most 9 tricks and the defenders are in control. Notice that (1)the defenders can take control in spite of a weak holding in trumps and (2) leading the stiff spade will not defeat the contract.

LINE OF DEFENSE - FORCING DECLARER

3.

| Contract: 6H |
| Lead: ? |

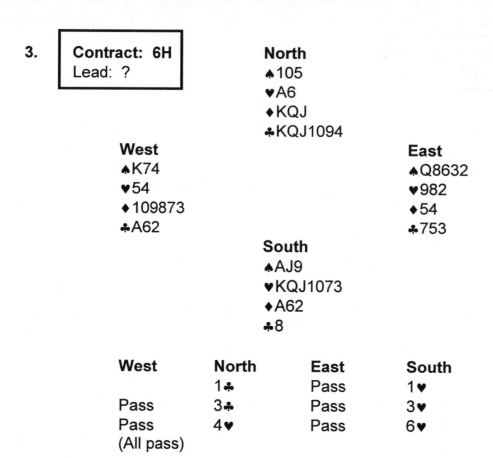

North
♠105
♥A6
♦KQJ
♣KQJ1094

West
♠K74
♥54
♦109873
♣A62

East
♠Q8632
♥982
♦54
♣753

South
♠AJ9
♥KQJ1073
♦A62
♣8

West	North	East	South
	1♣	Pass	1♥
Pass	3♣	Pass	3♥
Pass	4♥	Pass	6♥
(All pass)			

Sitting West, what is your line of defense?

Go active with the ♠4. You know from the bidding that as soon as trumps are drawn, declarer will knock out your ♣A and pitch his losers on the club suit. You must attack with the closest thing to a trick. If declarer had the ♠A and Q, nothing has been lost. Your spade trick was going away anyway.

LINE OF DEFENSE - ACTIVE

4.

Contract: 5H
Lead: ?

North
♠A8
♥J62
♦J104
♣AJ1065

West
♠QJ10742
♥95
♦Q73
♣KQ

East
♠K965
♥74
♦A952
♣972

South
♠3
♥AKQ1083
♦K86
♣843

West	North	East	South
			1♥
1♠	2♣	3♠	4♥
Pass	Pass	4♠	Pass
Pass	5♥	(All pass)	

Sitting West, what is your line of defense?

Go active with the ♦3. From the bidding it is clear that declarer has a club suit on the side and that your club honors are poorly placed. The declarer will give you your one club trick and then throw his losers away on the remaining clubs. If your partner has the ♠A instead of the ♦A, it will still be good when you get in with your club trick.

LINE OF DEFENSE - ACTIVE

5.

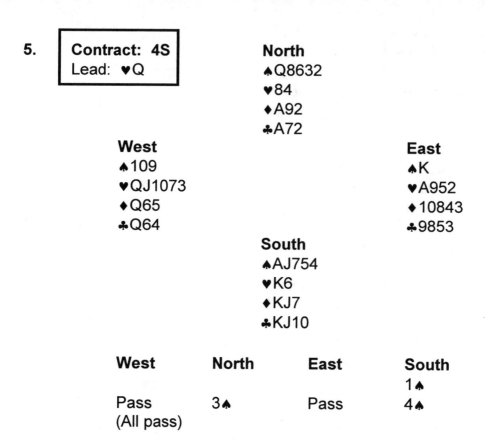

North
♠Q8632
♥84
♦A92
♣A72

West
♠109
♥QJ1073
♦Q65
♣Q64

East
♠K
♥A952
♦10843
♣9853

South
♠AJ754
♥K6
♦KJ7
♣KJ10

West	North	East	South
			1♠
Pass	3♠	Pass	4♠
(All pass)			

You take your partner's ♥Q with the ace. What is your line of defense?

Lead passively, continue hearts. There is no way any tricks can go away. However, if you switch to a club you eliminate declarer's guess on the queen's location. A switch to a diamond would be even worse - declarer would get three diamond tricks instead of two.

LINE OF DEFENSE - PASSIVE

6.

| Contract: 1NT |
| Lead: ? |

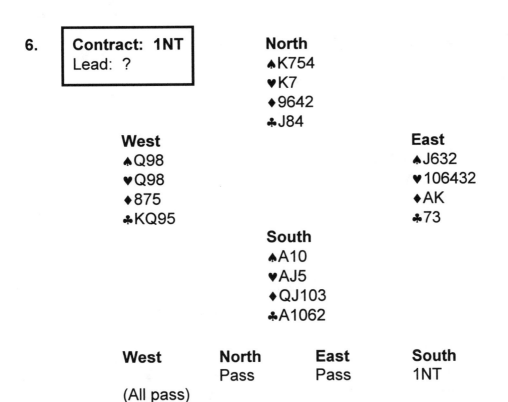

North
♠K754
♥K7
♦9642
♣J84

West
♠Q98
♥Q98
♦875
♣KQ95

East
♠J632
♥106432
♦AK
♣73

South
♠A10
♥AJ5
♦QJ103
♣A1062

West	North	East	South
	Pass	Pass	1NT

(All pass)

What is your line of defense?

Lead passively, the ♦8. With balanced hands and poor suits, stay passive. An aggressive lead from any one of the other 3 suits will give up a trick.

LINE OF DEFENSE - PASSIVE

7.

Contract: 5C(DBL)
Lead: ?

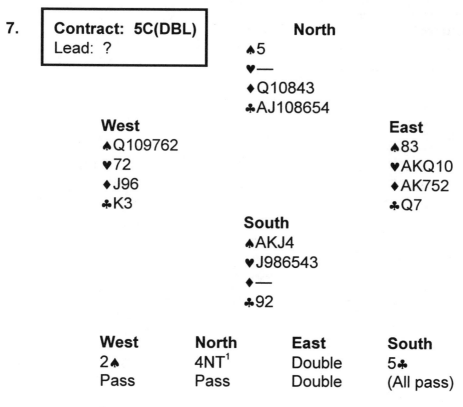

North
♠5
♥—
♦Q10843
♣AJ108654

West
♠Q109762
♥72
♦J96
♣K3

East
♠83
♥AKQ10
♦AK752
♣Q7

South
♠AKJ4
♥J986543
♦—
♣92

West	North	East	South
2♠	4NT[1]	Double	5♣
Pass	Pass	Double	(All pass)

[1]Shows minor suits

What is your line of defense?

Cut down declarer's ruffing power and lead the ♣3! North's 4NT bid showed a two-suited minor hand and South took a mere preference. They are sacrificing against you. Your partner has shown a strong hand and between the two of you all 3 other suits are well under control. Any other lead allows declarer to escape with down one. The point is to let the proper line of defense dictate the lead, no matter how unattractive it seems. The worst that can usually happen is an even exchange - loss of a trump trick for a saved ruffing trick.

LINE OF DEFENSE - CUTTING DOWN RUFFING POWER

8.

| Contract: 3H |
| Lead: ? |

North
♠QJ73
♥AQ1086
♦K8
♣32

West
♠K1086
♥K42
♦QJ106
♣J4

East
♠A94
♥53
♦93
♣AQ10985

South
♠52
♥J97
♦A7542
♣K76

West	North	East	South
Pass	2♦[1]	Pass	2♥
Pass	Pass	3♣	3♥
(All pass)			

[1]Flannery (5 hearts, 4 spades)

What is your line of defense?

Do not lead partner's suit. Do not lead your diamond sequence. Instead, cut down declarer's ruffing power by leading the trump 2. South has taken a mere preference following North's two-suited Flannery bid. West can see that South will be ruffing North's spade losers and he (West) will have to follow suit helplessly. Trump leads at every opportunity will hold the declarer to his contract and create a great result for you. Otherwise, declarer makes an extra trick.

LINE OF DEFENSE - CUTTING DOWN RUFFING POWER

9.

Contract: 4H
Lead: ♣2

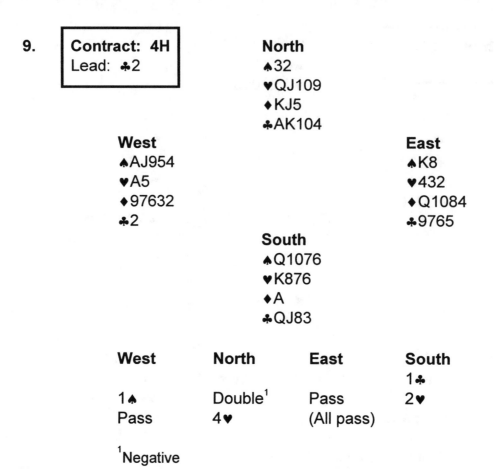

North
♠32
♥QJ109
♦KJ5
♣AK104

West
♠AJ954
♥A5
♦97632
♣2

East
♠K8
♥432
♦Q1084
♣9765

South
♠Q1076
♥K876
♦A
♣QJ83

West	North	East	South
			1♣
1♠	Double[1]	Pass	2♥
Pass	4♥	(All pass)	

[1] Negative

Declarer wins your club lead with dummy's ace; partner plays the 9 and declarer the 3. Declarer starts on trumps and you win the ace. What is your lead at trick three?

Either lead the ♠A (followed by a small spade) or underlead the ace. Partner heard South's club bid and knew your ♣2 was a singleton. His ♣9 was suit preference for spades.

LINE OF DEFENSE - CREATING TRUMP TRICKS

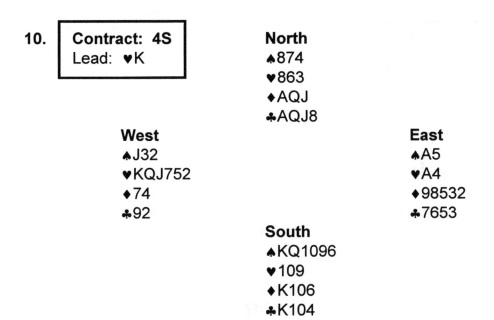

10.

Contract: 4S
Lead: ♥K

North
♠874
♥863
♦AQJ
♣AQJ8

West
♠J32
♥KQJ752
♦74
♣92

East
♠A5
♥A4
♦98532
♣7653

South
♠KQ1096
♥109
♦K106
♣K104

Your partner opens a weak 2H bid and the opponents proceed to 4S. Partner leads the ♥K. What is your line of defense?

In view of partner's weak 2H bid, the only chance to defeat the contract (a last resort) is by a trump promotion. Overtake the king and lead back a heart. Ruff the third heart with your trump ace and you have magically created a trick for your partner. You may have been among many defenders out there who were reluctant to ruff with trump aces - but no more!

LINE OF DEFENSE - CREATING TRUMP TRICKS

11.

Contract: 4S
Lead: ?

North
♠KJ103
♥AQ82
♦75
♣KJ9

West
♠A7
♥J54
♦J1092
♣A863

East
♠642
♥K1096
♦Q843
♣75

South
♠Q985
♥73
♦AK6
♣Q1042

West	North	East	South
	1♣	Pass	1♠
Pass	2♠	Pass	3♣
Pass	4♠	(All pass)	

What is your line of defense?

Go for a ruffing trick. The bidding suggests that the opponents have lots of clubs, so lead the ace and another club. Later, when you win your trump ace, give partner a ruff.

LINE OF DEFENSE - CREATING TRUMP TRICKS

12.

Contract: 4H
Lead: ♠A

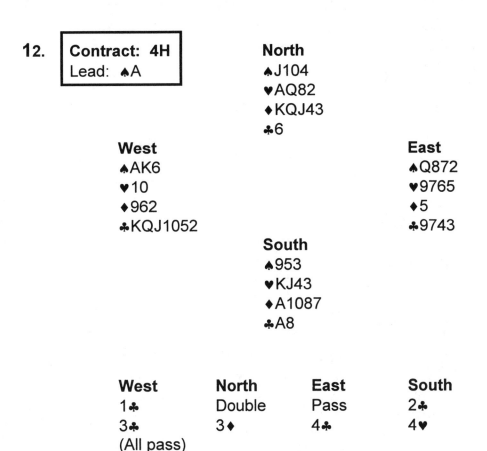

North
♠J104
♥AQ82
♦KQJ43
♣6

West
♠AK6
♥10
♦962
♣KQJ1052

East
♠Q872
♥9765
♦5
♣9743

South
♠953
♥KJ43
♦A1087
♣A8

West	North	East	South
1♣	Double	Pass	2♣
3♣	3♦	4♣	4♥
(All pass)			

Your partner takes the ♠A and K and leads to your queen; everybody follows. What next?

Lead your last spade and hope partner can uppercut the declarer (weaken his trump suit) and promote a trump trick in your hand. Incidentally, partner would have taken the ♣A if he had it. When there are no other options for a trick, this is a dandy!

LINE OF DEFENSE - CREATING TRUMP TRICKS

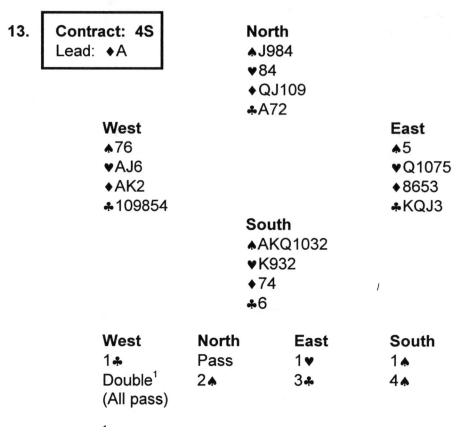

13.

Contract: 4S	
Lead: ♦A	

North
♠J984
♥84
♦QJ109
♣A72

West
♠76
♥AJ6
♦AK2
♣109854

East
♠5
♥Q1075
♦8653
♣KQJ3

South
♠AKQ1032
♥K932
♦74
♣6

West	North	East	South
1♣	Pass	1♥	1♠
Double¹	2♠	3♣	4♠
(All pass)			

¹Support double

After opening the ♦A, you switch to the ♣10. Declarer rises with the ace and partner drops the king, showing a sequence. Declarer plays trumps twice; your partner shows out on the second trump trick. Declarer then tables a small diamond and you take your king. What next?

Don't panic. Stay passive and lead a diamond or a club. Declarer has 6 spades, 2 diamonds and a club trick. Where is he going to get his 10th trick, unless you give it to him? It really pays to count!

LINE OF DEFENSE - PASSIVE

14.

| Contract: 4S |
| Lead: ♥5 |

North
♠ J10743
♥ 83
♦ K952
♣ Q7

West
♠ 8
♥ KJ952
♦ Q7
♣ 98543

East
♠ 965
♥ A106
♦ J84
♣ KJ62

South
♠ AKQ2
♥ Q74
♦ A1063
♣ A10

West	North	East	South
			1♠
Pass	2♠	Pass	3NT
Pass	4♠	(All pass)	

As East, you take the ♥A and return partner's lead. He wins the jack and switches to the ♣9. Dummy plays the ♣7, you the jack and declarer the ace. Declarer draws trumps in three rounds (partner shows out after one) and plays the ♥Q, partner covers with the K and the trick is ruffed in dummy. He then leads the ♣Q from the dummy and drops the 10 on your king. What is your next play?

Lead a club and give declarer a ruff and sluff! South is marked with 4 spades, 3 hearts and most likely 2 clubs. With 4 diamonds in his hand a sluff will do him no good (and you no harm). On the other hand, breaking that suit may give declarer the contract.

The bottom line is stay passive unless you see signs that your trick(s) will go away. On this hand counting told you the setting trick will not disappear. And, your partner will be in awe of your clever defense!

LINE OF DEFENSE - PASSIVE

15.

Contract: 5C
Lead: ♥A

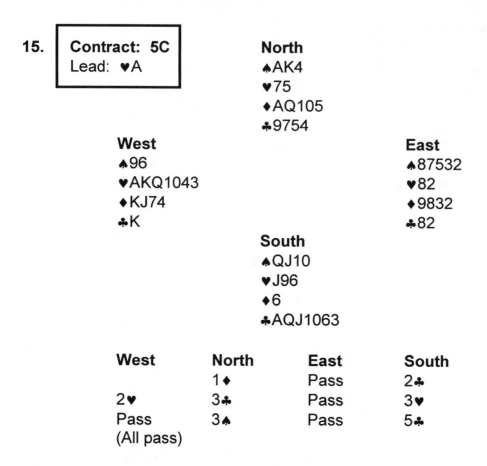

North
♠AK4
♥75
♦AQ105
♣9754

West
♠96
♥AKQ1043
♦KJ74
♣K

East
♠87532
♥82
♦9832
♣82

South
♠QJ10
♥J96
♦6
♣AQJ1063

West	North	East	South
	1♦	Pass	2♣
2♥	3♣	Pass	3♥
Pass	3♠	Pass	5♣
Pass			
(All pass)			

After overcalling the suit, partner leads the ♥A (from AK). What do you do with your yarborough?

The expert would not encourage a ruff in this particular situation. He can not overruff dummy's ♣9 and failure to do so would give away the position of any trump honor in his partner's hand (in this case the setting trick).

LINE OF DEFENSE - CREATING TRUMP TRICKS

16. Contract: 4S
Lead: ♦2

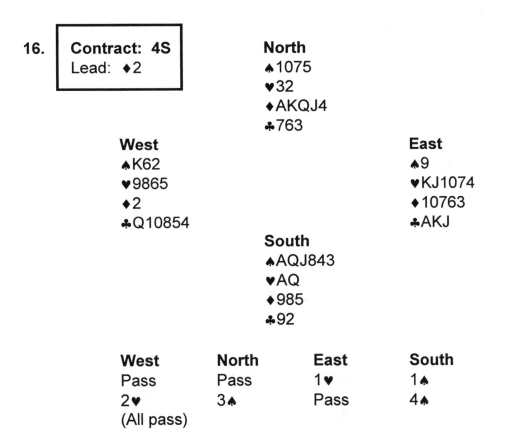

North
♠1075
♥32
♦AKQJ4
♣763

West
♠K62
♥9865
♦2
♣Q10854

East
♠9
♥KJ1074
♦10763
♣AKJ

South
♠AQJ843
♥AQ
♦985
♣92

West	North	East	South
Pass	Pass	1♥	1♠
2♥	3♠	Pass	4♠
(All pass)			

You lead your stiff diamond, dummy wins, East plays the 3 and declarer the 5. Declarer finesses the trump king and you win. How should you continue?

Do not lead your partner's heart suit. He read your lead and his ♦3 is suit preference for clubs, the lower ranking of the two remaining suits. Lead a high spot card in clubs, the 8, showing no interest in that suit. Partner will return diamonds twice for ruffs (down two).

LINE OF DEFENSE - CREATING TRUMP TRICKS

17.	**Contract: 6NT** Lead: ♥10	**North** ♠KJ1065 ♥AQJ6 ♦— ♣6532	

West
♠A32
♥1098532
♦872
♣J

East
♠Q987
♥4
♦J963
♣9874

South
♠4
♥K7
♦AKQ1054
♣AKQ10

West	North	East	South
	1♠	Pass	3♦
Pass	3♥	Pass	4NT
Pass	5♦	Pass	6NT
(All pass)			

The declarer won your partner's heart lead with his king, laid down three top diamonds and then gave you your jack. Playing standard signals, West followed three times with the ♦2, 8, and 7 and then discarded the ♥9. Declarer discarded three clubs and a spade from the dummy. It is your play.

Lead a spade; otherwise, declarer's losers will go away on hearts. How do you know? Partner screamed twice for a spade lead. First, he gave count with the ♦2, then played a higher and lower diamond at trick 3 and 4, asking for the higher ranking of the obvious suits. Secondly, he played the ♥9, urging the same. Normally this would signal attitude for hearts, but partner's opening lead of the ♥10 and the heart honors you see in dummy make it patently clear that partner cannot want a heart return. As you can see, neither a club nor a spade discard by partner would have done the trick because he didn't have the right spots (playing standard signals).

LINE OF DEFENSE - ACTIVE

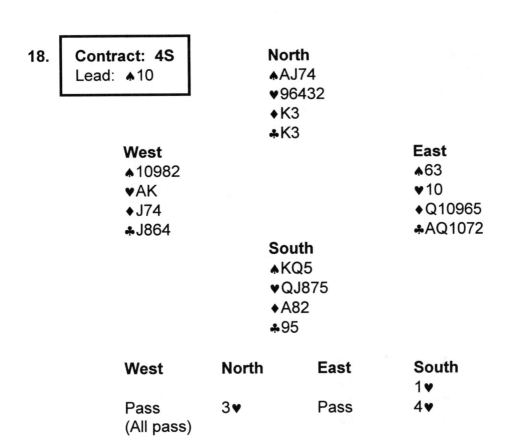

18.

Contract: 4S
Lead: ♠10

North
♠AJ74
♥96432
♦K3
♣K3

West
♠10982
♥AK
♦J74
♣J864

East
♠63
♥10
♦Q10965
♣AQ1072

South
♠KQ5
♥QJ875
♦A82
♣95

West	North	East	South
			1♥
Pass	3♥	Pass	4♥
(All pass)			

On your spade lead declarer plays the ace and your partner follows with the 3 (you are playing standard signals). Declarer plays a trump to your king; how do you continue?

Lay down the trump ace (partner can only have one trump) and find out which of the minor suits he prefers. In view of partner's discouraging signal in spades, there is a danger that declarer has 4 spade tricks and will throw off a minor suit loser. It's time to cash out!

LINE OF DEFENSE - ACTIVE

19.

| Contract: 4S |
| Lead: ♥2 |

North
♠ J3
♥ K9
♦ KQJ1062
♣ KJ7

West
♠ 754
♥ J862
♦ 75
♣ 8643

East
♠ A2
♥ AQ104
♦ 943
♣ Q1092

South
♠ KQ10986
♥ 753
♦ A8
♣ A5

West	North	East	South
	1♦	Pass	1♠
Pass	2♦	Pass	3♠[1]
Pass	4♠	(All pass)	

[1]Forcing

Your partner starts the attack with his fourth best heart, the two. You take the ♥Q and lead what?

Switch to the trump 2. This prevents declarer from ruffing a third heart, while retaining control of the trump suit. If declarer counters by trying to pitch heart losers on his diamond suit, partner will ruff the third one and you will have 4 tricks - 2 trumps and 2 hearts. If declarer leads another heart, instead, you win, cash your trump ace and take a third heart for down one.

This hand, taken from Sheinwold's syndicated column illustrates the importance of analyzing the dummy after the opening lead and the need once in a while for using more than one line of defense.

TWO LINES OF DEFENSE

- **Active** due to the threat of the running diamond suit, and

- **Trump lead** to cut declarer off from ruffing an immediate heart loser.

20.

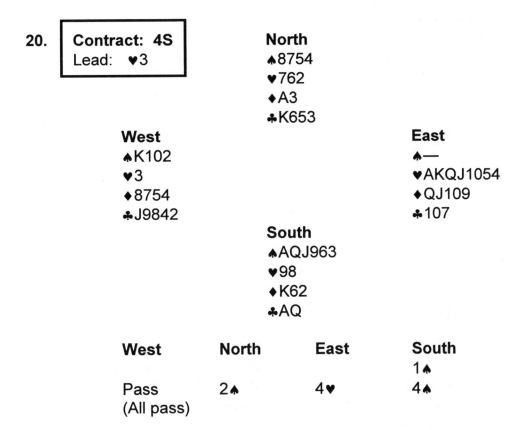

North
♠8754
♥762
♦A3
♣K653

West
♠K102
♥3
♦8754
♣J9842

East
♠—
♥AKQJ1054
♦QJ109
♣107

South
♠AQJ963
♥98
♦K62
♣AQ

West	North	East	South
			1♠
Pass	2♠	4♥	4♠
(All pass)			

This is one of those cases where the lead is obvious, the stiff ♥3 (your partner's suit). Partner takes the trick and leads two more rounds. But, declarer ruffs the third round with his ♠Q. Your play?

Pitch something and automatically *create* a second trump trick. Declarer's ruff with the ♠Q at trick three weakened his trump holding to the point that if you patiently wait and discard something, you will now have two trump tricks instead of one. And, you will defeat the contract.

LINE OF DEFENSE - CREATING TRUMP TRICKS

21.

Contract: 3S
Lead: ♦K

North
- ♠ QJ10
- ♥ 542
- ♦ A10
- ♣ KQJ76

West
- ♠ A942
- ♥ K108
- ♦ KQJ96
- ♣ A

East
- ♠ 6
- ♥ Q963
- ♦ 8543
- ♣ 10842

South
- ♠ K8753
- ♥ AJ7
- ♦ 72
- ♣ 953

West	North	East	South
	1♣	Pass	1♠
Double	2♠	Pass	Pass
3♦	Pass	Pass	3♠
(All pass)			

Declarer takes your ♦K with dummy's ace and leads the ♠Q which you duck. He leads the ♠J, your partner pitches off a diamond, and you duck again. If declarer leads another spade you will take the ace, force declarer with diamonds and eventually take control. But, declarer foils your efforts and leads the ♣K. Partner plays a low one (upside down signals) and you win your ace. You return a low heart and partner's queen goes to declarer's ace. Declarer finally leads the third round of trumps and you take your ace. Can you still defeat the contract? How?

Very possibly. Partner's count signal (low club) shows 4 clubs. He refused to part with one and may very well have the ♣10. If so, declarer has just 8 tricks (4 spades, 1 heart, 1 diamond, and 2 clubs). If you keep counting and don't panic, you will realize that you can defeat the contract by taking your ♠A and returning a diamond. Just sit back and wait for your two heart tricks. Solving this problem required:

- Forcing declarer
- Holding up your trump ace
- Signalling count

- Counting distribution
- Counting tricks
- Being passive
- **WHEW!**

TWO LINES OF DEFENSE - FORCING

- PASSIVE

Chapter 5

HOW TO PICK THE RIGHT OPENING LEAD*

Opening leads are an integral part of the defense and one of the most challenging aspects of bridge because they are based on so little information. Much of the time defenders are guessing what to lead. The purpose of this chapter is to reduce your guesswork to as few deals as possible.

The opening lead initiates one of your **five primary lines of defense.** At times, it will make or break the entire defense. At other times no lead is helpful. Declarer has so many tricks and there is nothing you can do to stop him. On still other hands there is too little information or clues from which to choose a line of defense or promising lead. Nevertheless, much of the time a useful - perhaps killing - lead can be found.

> **"Even the best-reasoned leads will be wrong some of the time ... opening leads are a little like the stock market. If you always do the right thing, you will win often but you won't win always. Do the best you can and suffer the occasional set back."**
> **- Mike Lawrence**

Once the dummy comes down, there may be time to recover (to reset the lead so to speak) and switch to the correct line of defense. Experts are able to find the **correct lead** or **switch** most of the time. If you will follow their thought process in Figure 5-1, eventually you will achieve the same degree of success.

***Notice:** Opening leads is a major subset of defense. You need to assimilate the key points in that chapter before reading this one.

How Experts Choose the Right Lead

THE FIVE LINES OF DEFENSE	THE RIGHT LEAD
1. Forcing declarer (conditions on page 55) 2. Being active (conditions on page 58)	Your partnership's strongest suit
3. Being passive (conditions on page 61)	Top of sequence or worthless suit
4. Cutting down ruffing power (conditions on page 65)	A trump
5. Creating trump tricks (conditions on page 71)	From or to shortness
Special Lead Situations	
• Gambling 3NTs	Aces, in the hope of finding declarer's weakness
• Notrump slams	Top of sequence or worthless suit
• Suit grand slams	A trump
• Special doubles - NT games/slams	Varies with bidding (see page 131)
- Suit games/slams	Unusual lead (see page 131)

Figure 5-1

CORRECT LINE OF DEFENSE DETERMINES THE OPENING LEAD

At the outset, the most important thing you can do to improve your leads is to simply think about them as the bidding proceeds and practice selecting the correct line of defense. The proper line of defense, in turn, will usually tell you what the opening lead should be except for some special lead situations which we will discuss later. The conditions for these lines of defense have all been discussed in the previous chapter (see Figure 5-1).

The particular leads that initiate three of the five lines of defense are self-evident. In passive situations you must find the suit that gives away nothing (or as little as possible) to declarer and forces him to guess where the cards are. To cut down ruffing power, a trump is the obvious lead. To create trump tricks of your own, you must lead from shortness or to perceived shortness in your partner's hand.

However, in the case of the two remaining lines of defense, forcing and active defenses, you must find your partnership's strongest suit. The answer may lie in *your own hand* (in which case you have no problem) or it may depend on *bidding inferences*.

> **"If you are going to be effective with your opening leads, you must know how to see through the bidding to find the best lead."**
> **- Mike Lawrence**

Bidding Inferences Will Reveal Your Strongest Suit

Inferences are often the key to finding the partnership's strongest suit. Some inferences come from your partner and others from the opponents. They could be negative in that you not only must listen to what is *said* during the auction but also to what goes *unsaid*.

For example, during the bidding process, there are numerous opportunities for partners to tell each other where their strength *is* or *is not*. You can tell your partner where your strength *is* by what is called "lead directors" and where your strength *is not* by *silence*. Typical lead directors are shown in Figure 5-2.

Lead Directors

- Overcalls

- Preempts

- Bid best minor

- Open third hand
  light for lead

- Lead-directing
  doubles

Figure 5-2

A partnership understanding about lead directors is important because any time such bids are omitted during an auction the strong implications are twofold. Either (1) partner does not have a suit worth bidding or (2) his suit is below the opponent's bid suit and he can not afford to bid it at the next higher level. In other words, the absence of a bid, especially when partner is known to have some values, suggests possible interest in a lower ranking suit that he couldn't conveniently bid.

One thing is for sure. The absence of any bid in Figure 5-2 strongly implies the need for some *other* lead.

Another good way to reveal the partnership's strongest suit is to double artificial bids. There are many opportunities during auctions to do this (see Figure 5-3).

Artificial Bids Which Can be Doubled to Reveal Your Strongest Suit

- Stayman

- Transfers

- New minor forcing

- Fourth suit forcing

- Cue bids

- Blackwood responses

Figure 5-3

Failure to double any of these artificial bids when they arise shows **no interest** in the suits bid and probably interest in some **other** suit. Doubles, on the other hand, suggest defensive tricks in that suit, not simply length. In short, if you listen carefully, you may be able to deduce the right lead through a process of elimination. To illustrate how this works, look at several bidding sequences and decide what you would do.

Illustration Number 1

Contract: 6S
Lead: ?

West	North	East	South
			1♠
Pass	4♠	Pass	4NT
Pass	5♦	Pass	5NT
Pass	6♣	Pass	6♠
(All pass)			

Partner had little chance to overcall but could have doubled either the 5D or 6C bids if he were interested in either of those two suits. So, unless you have an obvious choice in your own hand, lead a heart.

Illustration Number 2

```
Contract: 3NT
Lead: ?
```

West	North	East	South
	1♦	Pass	1NT
Pass	3NT		

If you are sitting West with just two or three points and no real suit of your own - consider trying to hit your partner. He has at least 10 points but did not overcall the 1D opening bid. That means his heart and spade holdings are relatively weak. If one of your major-suit holdings looks very attractive, then lead that suit. Otherwise, you should lead a club - the suit your partner was not able to overcall at the one level.

Illustration Number 3

```
Contract: 3NT
Lead: ?
```

West
♠873
♥K10742
♦ —
♣K8632

West	North	East	South
	Pass	Pass	1NT
Pass	2♣	Pass	2♠
Pass	3NT	(All pass)	

Based on inferences from the bidding, what should West lead? Had the bidding gone 1NT - 3NT, a heart lead would have been appropriate.

However, North's bidding clearly shows interest in a major suit and he rejected South's spades, so he must have hearts. Your hearts are in a poor position in front of the dummy, therefore, lead a club. The full deal:

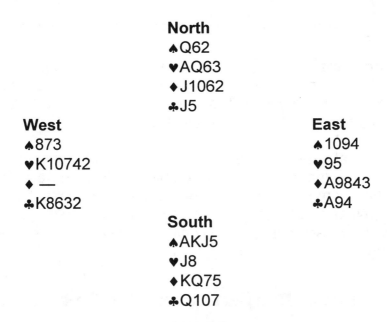

North
♠Q62
♥AQ63
♦J1062
♣J5

West
♠873
♥K10742
♦ —
♣K8632

East
♠1094
♥95
♦A9843
♣A94

South
♠AKJ5
♥J8
♦KQ75
♣Q107

We hope these illustrations prove to you that it is essential for you and your partner to have a solid understanding about inferences that flow from the bidding process and, more importantly, from the all-important omissions - ***the bids that were not made***. Moreover, if you really want a particular lead, you need to follow the expert advice in Chapter 2 and get your bid in early. Remember, ***if you do not take action to suggest a defensive lead when you have the opportunity to do so, partner will assume you have no interest in seeing that suit led.***

SPECIAL NOTRUMP CONSIDERATIONS

There are fewer things to consider when deciding what to lead against a notrump contract. The lines of defense are limited - either active or passive. As a general rule, experts make active leads when their suits are good (the standard lead against notrump contracts) and passive leads when their best suits are weak and only 4 cards in length.

The tendency also is to stay passive when the opponents have had a misfit auction or when declarer is powerful and dummy is weak. On the other hand, the tendency is to get busy and take your tricks when the bidding suggests long running suits or slam interest.

Entries are vital when defending against notrump contracts. Therefore, when you have most of your partnership's points, try to establish your hand. When partner has most of the outstanding points, try to establish his hand. When you have no obvious lead of your own against notrump contracts, there are some other well-understood lead preferences as shown in Figure 5-4.

Other Lead Preferences Against Notrump Contracts

- If no entries, try to hit partner.
- Unbid majors in preference to a minor.
- A suit partner was not able to overcall conveniently.
- When you have good spot cards, take advantage of your positional strength by leading up to declarer's suit rather than through dummy's bid suit.

Figure 5-4

The next hand illustrates the common lead problem in notrump contracts - whether you should go "active" or "passive."

```
┌─────────────────────────┐
│ Contract:  3NT          │
│ Lead:  ?                │
└─────────────────────────┘
```

West
♠KJ9
♥KJ65
♦974
♣KQ6

West	**North**	**East**	**South**
			1NT
Pass	3NT	(All pass)	

According to the bidding, the offense has about 26 points. You (as West) have 13 points, which leaves your partner with next to nothing. You have no real suit of your own so an attacking lead would be useless. A passive lead of the ♦7 gives the declarer no gift and forces him to do all of his own work. The full deal:

North
♠Q76
♥1098
♦AK52
♣J108

West
♠KJ9
♥KJ65
♦974
♣KQ6

East
♠543
♥732
♦J86
♣9752

South
♠A1082
♥AQ4
♦Q103
♣A43

SPECIAL LEADS FOR SPECIAL SITUATIONS

There are a number of special or conventional leads associated with particular auctions that are used widely by experts.

Against Gambling 3NTs

- Lead an ace. Take a good look at both dummy and your partner's signal and try to find your partnership's strongest suit immediately.

Against 6 or 7 Notrump Contracts

- Lead passively and try to disguise your honor card holdings and distribution.

Against Grand Slam Suit Contracts

- Lead a trump and again try to give declarer no information on your holdings and distribution.

Against Doubled Low-level Suit Contracts

- Stop declarer from taking ruffing tricks he doesn't deserve. Exhaust his trumps to the extent you can with trump leads (see page 67).

Against Doubled Game and Slam Contracts

When the opponents own the cards, experts do not double confidently bid games or slams without special reason. When they do, it is usually a *lead-directing double*. There are different guidelines depending on whether the double applies to a *notrump* or *suit* contract.

In *notrump* contracts the meaning of a lead-directing double varies with the bidding. Figure 5-5 shows the different meanings agreed to by some experts.

What Do Lead-directing Doubles Mean Against Notrump Games/Slams?

The Bidding	Meaning of Double
• Neither defender has bid and your partner doubled	Lead dummy's first bid suit.
• Only partner has bid and he doubled	Lead partner's suit.
• Only you have bid and your partner doubled	Lead your suit.
• Both of you have bid	Lead suit of the stronger hand (for entries).
• No suits have been bid (eg. 1NT-3NT)	Lead your shortest major.

Figure 5-5

A further discussion of the doubles in Figure 5-5 can be found in the next chapter on "When and When Not to Double" (see p. 161).

In high-level *suit* contracts, where ruffing can quickly defeat the opponents, the lead-directing double calls for an unusual lead. This excludes trumps and any suit bid by you or your partner. Often, it suggests shortness (void) in the doubler's hand, and it is up to the opening leader to figure out which suit.

Illustrations of these lead-directing doubles can be found in the next chapter. They happen fairly infrequently, but they do come up often enough to justify including them in your partnership understandings. And, when they do occur, you will be in for a good result.

TYPES OF LEADS

Figure 5-6 displays the types of leads most frequently used by the top players. The bottom line is that usually you can do well with any of these lead types *if* you are able to diagnose the correct line of defense for the particular hand.

Types of Leads Most Frequently Used

TYPE	APPLICATION
• Fourth best	Use favored against notrump contracts.
• Third from even, low from odd	Use favored against suit contracts.
• Attitude	The lower the spot card, the better you like the suit. Use favored against notrump contracts.
• Zero or two higher	Use favored against both suit and notrump contracts

Figure 5-6

If you are interested in knowing more about what specific card to play from various holdings once you have chosen a suit to lead, a recent book on opening leads addresses this subject in detail (see Chapter 10).

A final thought. You will find that the amount of guesswork you do will often vary with the bidding. Strong and revealing auctions will make your work on opening leads much easier. Weak and uninformed ones may put you on the guess more than you would like.

> **"The difference between informative auctions and uninformative auctions is brutal. Be sure to listen to the bidding and use all the information that is there."**
>
> **- Mike Lawrence**

– – – – – –

Now if you are well versed in the five lines of defense and in how to make killing leads, you are in a sound position to double your opponents more often when they start pushing you around - the subject of our next chapter. Further, now that you have become tough defenders, your opponents will *not be happy* to see you arrive at the table. Instead, you will be the opponents they would rather avoid. To prove this to yourself, try the following quiz.

The answers to these problems begin on page 142. They assume you have read both Chapter 4 on how the experts approach the defense of a bridge hand and this one on opening leads.

The question on each hand is the same - what is your opening lead? Before answering that question, be careful to associate your opening lead with a particular line of defense or special lead situation, using both bidding inferences and information in your own hand. If you get fewer than 10 correct, you need to go back and read over these two chapters again. If you get 10-12 correct, you are becoming a real threat on defense. If you do even better, you can retire and write your own book!

1.

| Contract: 4S |
| Lead: ? |

West
♠32
♥KJ2
♦765
♣87653

West	North	East	South
	1♦	Pass	1♠
Pass	3♦	Pass	3♠
Pass	4♠	(All pass)	

2.

Contract: 4S
Lead: ?

West
♠654
♥AQ108
♦76
♣QJ109

West	North	East	South
			1♠
Pass	2♦	Pass	2♥
Pass	2♠	Pass	3♥
Pass	4♠	(All pass)	

3.

Contract: 4H
Lead: ?

West
♠AJ73
♥A64
♦6
♣A6532

West	North	East	South
			1NT
Pass	2♣	Pass	2♥
Pass	4♥	(All pass)	

4.

Contract: 4S
Lead: ?

West
♠93
♥A7642
♦K1053
♣86

West	North	East	South
	1♣	Pass	1♠
Pass	3♣	Pass	3♠
Pass	4♠	(All pass)	

5.

Contract: 3NT
Lead: ?

West
♠Q6542
♥J754
♦8
♣AK3

West	North	East	South
	3♦	Pass	3NT
(All pass)			

6.

Contract: 4H
Lead: ?

West
♠ J10
♥ K753
♦ KJ942
♣ 82

West	North	East	South
			1♥
Pass	2♥	Pass	4♥
(All pass)			

7.

Contract: 3NT(DBL)
Lead: ?

Which suit would you lead against each of the following auctions?

Bidding - Case A

West	North	East	South
			1♣
Pass	1♥	Pass	1NT
Pass	2NT	Pass	3NT
Pass	Pass	Double	(All pass)

Bidding - Case B

West	North	East	South
			1♣
Pass	1♥	1♠	1NT
Pass	2NT	Pass	3NT
Pass	Pass	Double	(All pass)

8.

Contract: 7H
Lead: ?

West
♠ QJ1095
♥ 84
♦ 96
♣ K643

West	North	East	South
	1♣	Pass	1♥
Pass	2♦	Pass	2♠
Pass	3♦	Pass	3♥
Pass	4♥	Pass	4NT
Pass	5♠	Pass	7♥
(All pass)			

9.

Contract: 4H
Lead: ?

West
♠ Q1053
♥ J1098
♦ 6
♣ A952

West	North	East	South
			1NT
Pass	2♣	Pass	2♥
Pass	4♥	(All pass)	

10.

Contract: **6D**
Lead: ?

West
♠Q63
♥97532
♦642
♣A7

West	North	East	South
			1♦
Pass	2♣	Pass	3♣
Pass	4♦	Pass	4NT
Pass	5♦	Pass	6♦
(All pass)			

11.

Contract: **4H**
Lead: ?

West
♠9642
♥842
♦6
♣J9743

West	North	East	South
			1NT
Pass	2♣	Pass	2♥
Pass	4♥	(All pass)	

12. **Contract: 3NT(DBL)**
Lead: ?

West
♠Q10932
♥KQ109
♦Q5
♣A6

West	North	East	South
1♠	2♣	Pass	2NT
Pass	3NT	Double	(All pass)

13. **Contract: 7S(DBL)**
Lead: ?

West
♠5
♥KJ87
♦87543
♣765

West	North	East	South
			1♦
Pass	2♣	4♥	4♠
5♥	6♠	7♥	Pass[1]
Pass	7♠	Double	(All pass)

[1]First round heart control, invites grand slam

14.

Contract: 3NT(DBL)
Lead: ?

West
♠53
♥J1094
♦10754
♣842

West	North	East	South
			1NT
Pass	3NT	Double	(All pass)

The opponents reached a 3NT game before your partner had a chance to bid. Then, he doubled! What is your lead?

ANSWERS TO CHAPTER 5 QUIZ

1.

Contract: 4S
Lead: ?

North
♠K4
♥876
♦AKQ1098
♣A10

West
♠32
♥KJ2
♦765
♣87653

East
♠QJ10
♥A543
♦432
♣Q42

South
♠A98765
♥Q109
♦J
♣KJ9

West	North	East	South
	1♦	Pass	1♠
Pass	3♦	Pass	3♠
Pass	4♠	(All pass)	

Lead the ♥2. Dummy has shown a strong diamond suit as well as trump support. You know from your own hand that the diamond suit will break well for the declarer. Time to be active. So, lead the closest thing you have to a trick. If the opponents have the missing heart honors, no problem - you were never scoring any heart tricks anyway.

LINE OF DEFENSE - ACTIVE

2.

Contract: 4S
Lead: ?

North
- ♠ A109
- ♥ 32
- ♦ AK432
- ♣ 432

West
- ♠ 654
- ♥ AQ108
- ♦ 76
- ♣ QJ109

East
- ♠ 32
- ♥ 97
- ♦ QJ1098
- ♣ K876

South
- ♠ KQJ87
- ♥ KJ654
- ♦ 5
- ♣ A5

West	North	East	South
			1♠
Pass	2♦	Pass	2♥
Pass	2♠	Pass	3♥
Pass	4♠	(All pass)	

Lead a trump. With such a strong holding in declarer's heart side suit you need to protect your tricks. Your hand suggests that the other side suit (diamonds) will break badly for declarer, too. Lead a trump every time you win a heart trick and you will defeat the game contract. Otherwise, declarer will give up two heart tricks, cash his 3 minor-suit tricks and cross ruff the entire hand for 11 tricks (one overtrick).

LINE OF DEFENSE - CUTTING DOWN RUFFING POWER

3.

Contract: 4H
Lead: ?

West
♠AJ73
♥A64
♦6
♣A6532

West	North	East	South
			1NT
Pass	2♣	Pass	2♥
Pass	4♥	(All pass)	

You didn't lead the ♦6, did you? Based on the bidding, partner has at most a jack and certainly no entry. A reasonable chance is that partner has a singleton or doubleton club. Try the ♣A and another club. Perhaps partner will be able to ruff now or later when you get in with your trump ace.

LINE OF DEFENSE - CREATING TRUMP TRICKS

4. | Contract: 4S
Lead: ?

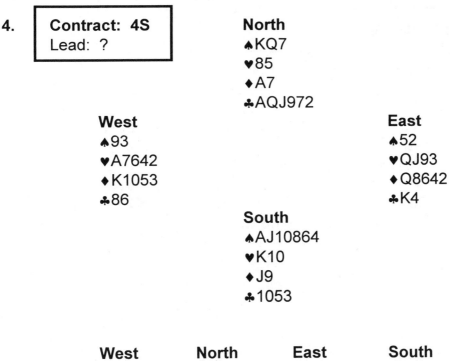

North
♠KQ7
♥85
♦A7
♣AQJ972

West
♠93
♥A7642
♦K1053
♣86

East
♠52
♥QJ93
♦Q8642
♣K4

South
♠AJ10864
♥K10
♦J9
♣1053

West	North	East	South
	1♣	Pass	1♠
Pass	3♣	Pass	3♠
Pass	4♠	(All pass)	

Lead a low diamond. North has shown with his jump rebid a long and strong club suit. Declarer will draw trumps and then pitch his losers as soon as the club suit is set up. You must develop your tricks now. It turns out you have one each in clubs and diamonds and 2 in hearts, *if* you collect them in time.

LINE OF DEFENSE - ACTIVE

5.

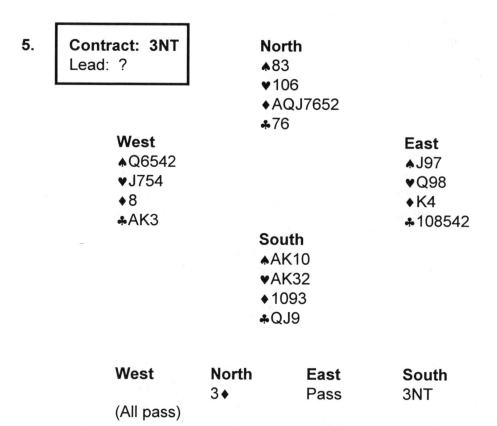

| Contract: 3NT |
| Lead: ? |

North
- ♠83
- ♥106
- ♦AQJ7652
- ♣76

West
- ♠Q6542
- ♥J754
- ♦8
- ♣AK3

East
- ♠J97
- ♥Q98
- ♦K4
- ♣108542

South
- ♠AK10
- ♥AK32
- ♦1093
- ♣QJ9

West	North	East	South
	3♦	Pass	3NT
(All pass)			

Lead a club honor asking for partner's attitude. On the bidding there is a real threat of a long running minor, so you must find your tricks quickly. If partner discourages you in clubs, you can try a major suit. As it turns out, partner will be delighted with your club lead.

LINE OF DEFENSE - ACTIVE

6.

> **Contract: 4H**
> Lead: ?

West
♠ J10
♥ K753
♦ KJ942
♣ 82

West	North	East	South
			1♥
Pass	2♥	Pass	4♥
(All pass)			

Lead a low diamond. With four trumps, your best chance of beating this contract is to force declarer and either create a second trump trick or take over control of the hand. When you have long trumps, lead your best suit or partner's suit. It will often start declarer on the road to ruin.

LINE OF DEFENSE - FORCING DECLARER

7.

Contract: 3NT(DBL)
Lead: ?

Which suit would you lead against each of the following auctions?

Bidding - Case A

West	North	East	South
			1♣
Pass	1♥	Pass	1NT
Pass	2NT	Pass	3NT
Pass	Pass	Double	(All pass)

Bidding - Case B

West	North	East	South
			1♣
Pass	1♥	1♠	1NT
Pass	2NT	Pass	3NT
Pass	Pass	Double	(All pass)

In case A, partner's double calls for dummy's 1st bid suit (hearts). It is a conventional lead. Partner is sitting there with a heart stack and believes he can beat the contract with a heart lead.

In case B, partner's double simply says he bid a good suit, has an entry, and if you lead his suit, he can defeat the contract. This action is a matter of partnership agreement.

LEAD-DIRECTING DOUBLE

Contract: 7H		
Lead: ?		

North
♠A
♥2
♦AK1072
♣AJ9852

West
♠QJ1095
♥84
♦96
♣K643

East
♠643
♥765
♦QJ43
♣Q107

South
♠K872
♥AKQJ1093
♦85
♣ —

West	North	East	South
	1♣	Pass	1♥
Pass	2♦	Pass	2♠
Pass	3♦	Pass	3♥
Pass	4♥	Pass	4NT
Pass	5♠	Pass	7♥
(All pass)			

Lead a trump - the most preferred lead on grand slams (unless you have a cashable ace)! The ♠Q from top of a sequence looks attractive. However, when defenders lack cashable tricks, the only way a natural trick can go away during the play of the hand is through declarer's ruffing power. In short, against grand slams a trump lead is usually the most effective lead and in this case, it is the only lead which defeats the contract.

SPECIAL SITUATION LEAD

9.

> **Contract: 4H**
> Lead: ?

West
♠Q1053
♥J1098
♦6
♣A952

West	North	East	South
			1NT
Pass	2♣	Pass	2♥
Pass	4♥	(All pass)	

Lead a low spade or the ♥J. It is tempting to lead your stiff diamond. However, it usually does not pay off to look for ruffs when you have natural trump trick(s). The chances of getting 2 ruffs are highly remote. The bidding did not reveal much about the hand. A spade lead may develop tricks in that suit and put you in position to force the declarer.

The ♥J is also an attractive lead because it would reduce declarer's ruffing power and make the declarer find the missing cards in the other suits himself.

This is one of those hands where analysis of the dummy (source of tricks, shortness, etc.) will help you find the correct line of defense.

LINE OF DEFENSE - SUBJECT TO DUMMY ANALYSIS

Contract: 6D
Lead: ?

West
♠Q63
♥97532
♦642
♣A7

West	North	East	South
			1♦
Pass	2♣	Pass	3♣
Pass	4♦	Pass	4NT
Pass	5♦	Pass	6♦
(All pass)			

Lead a small spade. The dummy will come down with a club suit and you know from the auction that declarer has support for that suit. As soon as your trumps are drawn and the declarer knocks out your ♣A, its "all over but the shouting" - his losers will go away on the club suit. The only chance you have is to develop a trick early. In these situations attack from your strongest values. To succeed in a suit where you are weak would require more from partner than you can reasonably expect.

LINE OF DEFENSE - ACTIVE

11.

West
♠9642
♥842
♦6
♣J9743

West	North	East	South
			1NT
Pass	2♣	Pass	2♥
Pass	4♥	(All pass)	

Lead your stiff diamond. Partner has all the outstanding cards. If partner can give you a ruff, watch carefully the card he returns for a suit-preference signal. Two ruffs may be the only way to beat the contract. In any event, trying for ruffs is best when no other line of defense is apparent.

LINE OF DEFENSE - CREATING TRUMP TRICKS

12.

> **Contract: 3NT(DBL)**
> Lead: ?

West
♠Q10932
♥KQ109
♦Q5
♣A6

West	North	East	South
1♠	2♣	Pass	2NT
Pass	3NT	Double	(All pass)

Lead a low spade. If partner had not doubled, you probably would have led the ♥Q, asking partner to drop the jack if he had it. But, partner's double changes everything. Partner is saying he has help for you in your suit and to please lead a spade.

LEAD-DIRECTING DOUBLE

13.

Contract: 7S(DBL)
Lead: ?

North
♠AJ107
♥9
♦A10
♣AJ9832

West
♠5
♥KJ87
♦87543
♣765

East
♠432
♥AQ1065432
♦ —
♣104

South
♠KQ986
♥ —
♦KQJ962
♣KQ

West	North	East	South
			1♦
Pass	2♣	4♥	4♠
5♥	6♠	7♥	Pass[1]
Pass	7♠	Double	(All pass)

[1]First round heart control, invites grand slam

Lead the ♦8. The bidding clearly shows it is the opponents' hand. Having pushed them to the seven level, your partnership should be very happy with a one-trick set. So, there is no need for partner to double unless he requires an unusual lead. An unusual lead automatically bars your own suit and trumps. So, you have to choose between the minors. You have longer diamonds, so that suit is most likely partner's void. Since you want the higher ranking suit returned, choose the ♦8.

Note: Because of your holding in the minors, it was relatively easy to pick the right opening lead. However, partner had the opportunity to make it easy for you regardless of your holding in the minor suits. Instead of bidding 7H he could have bid 7D. It never hurts to throw in a lead-directing bid, when obvious, during the auction.

LEAD-DIRECTING DOUBLE

14.

Contract: 3NT(DBL)
Lead: ?

West
♠53
♥J1094
♦10754
♣842

West	North	East	South
			1NT
Pass	3NT	Double	(All pass)

The opponents reached a 3NT game before your partner had a chance to bid. Then, he doubled! What is your lead?

Lead the ♠5. When partner doubles this kind of auction it doesn't mean he has lots of high cards. Rather, he has a source of tricks but could not get into the bidding. The doubler's purpose is to warn you off your normal lead. It asks for your shortest major without a top honor.

LEAD-DIRECTING DOUBLE

Chapter 6

WHEN AND WHEN NOT TO DOUBLE

The advent of the negative double, responsive double, support double and cooperative double have all seemingly detracted from the penalty double. In reality, this is not true. The penalty double is still one of the strongest weapons in the game of bridge, especially when used under the proper circumstances.

The tendency of the average bridge player is to double more often as the auction escalates to higher levels. The problem with this is that in return for a very small profit, the double may reveal just enough information to allow the declarer to make the contract or, worse still, to escape to a better one. Experts, on the other hand, generally reserve their most effective doubles in matchpoints for partscore battles. Unless it's their hand, expert doubles at higher levels are triggered by specific exceptions.

Penalty Doubles by Experts

Contract Level	When Experts Double
• Partscores	• Often
• Games/Slams	• Specific exceptions
• The Five Level	• Their 5-level contract is doubtful or penalty more attractive.

Figure 6-1

PARTSCORE DOUBLES

Fierce partscore battles are waged at matchpoints. In tough events, such battles frequently lead to doubled contracts. Many matchpoints hang in the balance. The experts follow this general rule: if it is your hand and you feel you are being pushed around, you ***must*** double the opponents or suffer a bad result. You must be willing to risk the possibility that the

157

doubled contract will make. The argument goes like this. If the opponents make their doubled contract, your score won't be much worse. But, if they don't, your reward will be much greater. An even more specific rule is:

> **"If the opponents are not making 1 in 5 of your doubles, you are not doubling enough."**
> **- Anonymous Expert**

When the opponents are vulnerable, doubles of partscore contracts are even more attractive because you are trying to get the "*Magic 200*," always a near top score. There are three good reasons why you should be aggressive and double the opponents in partscore situations.

1. Double when you have reason to believe it is your hand and the opponents are pushing you above your makeable contract level (see Law of Total Tricks page 10).

2. Double when there are misfits. A double will warn your partner and likely avoid a minus score. For example, the opponents may be setting up (baiting) your partner with one more round of bidding. Partner needs to be warned of the misfit and of the trap being set.

3. Double when you have some extra values or feel that it is your hand but do not know exactly whether to bid on or to defend and wish to consult your partner. Partner will pull the double if he has been bidding more on distribution than high card points or if he is longer in your trump suit than previously promised. These doubles allow flexibility and are referred to as "Cooperative Doubles." On occasion, there is a bonus - you are allowed to play the hand at a lower level or undoubled. (Either you scared the opponents off with your penalty-oriented double, or if partner had to pull it, they let you play your contract unmolested.)

A good system of partnership doubling at partscore levels pays off big in matchpoints. And, when one of these doubles backfires, keep this in mind.

> **"Neither you nor your opponents will always make the perfect decision. Be willing to take advantage when an opponent makes the wrong choice. If you spend a lifetime finding something to fret about, you will not have any minus 670's or minus 500's - - but you won't have a winning game, either."**
>
> **- Mike Lawrence**

Experience is the best teacher because it develops the fine judgment needed in the delicate partscore situations. In general, it pays to be aggressive. The only time experts shy away from partscore doubles is when their hands are distributional or there is too much length in partner's suit. Here are a couple of illustrations of partscore doubles.

Illustration No. 1

Vul: None

South
♠4
♥Q975
♦AKJ864
♣A4

West	North	East	South
			1♦
Pass	1♠	Pass	2♦
Pass	Pass	2♥	?

East has balanced in with an unsafe suit (see page 15). Double on the grounds of a misfit. Misfits will always produce more defensive tricks than normal because the misfit suit will generate both high card winners and defensive ruffing tricks. In this particular case, if partner has little in the way of defensive values or too many of your diamonds, he can pull the double, and probably you will play 3 diamonds undoubled.

Illustration No. 2

	Vul: East/West			**South**
				♠963
				♥K764
				♦K73
				♣A97

West	North	East	South
	Pass	1♦	Pass
1NT	Double	Pass	2♥
3♦	Pass	Pass	?

The high card points are evenly divided between you and the opponents. The issue here is should you as South pass, go to three hearts or double the opponents. Due to favorable vulnerability and a fit, a sacrifice at the 3 level is a viable option. But, rather than make a unilateral decision to go beyond the Law of Total Tricks level (see page 10), it is wise to consult partner first. If you double, he may have enough defensive values and the proper shape to sit - the final decision is his.*

Reputation as a Doubler Is Essential

Once your partnership develops the reputation for making close partscore doubles, three things will happen - all good. You will get less interference in your auctions. You will be allowed to play more contracts (and go plus). You will be allowed to play contracts at lower levels (which adds up to a lot more matchpoints).

---

*Although in rare situations your double might have been "penalty," the flexibility needed in partscore battles makes it more advantageous to play these kinds of doubles as "cooperative" (see page 239).

GAME/SLAM DOUBLES

Experts rarely double games and slams confidently bid.* There are three exceptions: hands breaking badly, sheer desperation, and, most productively, for lead direction.

Exception #1 - Hands Breaking Badly

Hands breaking badly can be doubled provided declarer has no escape route. But the bad breaks have to indeed be a nasty surprise - a solid stack against the declarer. The worst thing you can do is give declarer just enough information to make the contract. You must think about alternative contracts before you pounce on this one. Many a declarer has escaped to a better contract and wound up taking advantage of the doubler in the play of the hand.

Exception #2 - Sheer Desperation

Sheer desperation is when you need a good board so much that you are willing to practice a little deception to get it. For example, you are void in declarer's trump suit and sense from the bidding that the opponents do not have a great fit or a sure contract. The idea is to get declarer off to a bad start and misguess the trump suit.

Exception #3 - Lead Directing

Lead directing is the best reason of all for penalty doubles. When the opponents own the cards and bid games and slams, a lead-directing double to tell partner what to lead can save the day. By using such a double you are telling partner that if he can find the right lead, the opponents will go down. Better still, partner will not have to guess. There are special understandings about what the right lead should be.

---

*This assumes, of course, that the deal belongs to the opponents and they are not trying to steal from you.

In the case of confidently bid *game* or *slam* contracts in *notrump*, such a double says:

- If neither you nor your partner has bid, lead *dummy's first bid suit*.

- If *your partner* has bid a suit and doubled, you should lead it.

- If *you* have bid a suit and partner has doubled, you should lead it.

- If *both of you* have bid a suit, lead the suit bid by the stronger hand because it has entries. This is a suggestion from Mike Lawrence's new book on opening leads.

- If no one has bid a suit (eg., 1NT-3NT), you should lead your *shortest major*.

These understandings are fairly well accepted among the experts. To illustrate the last one, you are East and the bidding goes:

```
┌─────────────────┐
│  Vul: Both      │
└─────────────────┘
```

East

♠64
♥AKQ106
♦J74
♣1043

West	North	East	South
			1NT
Pass	3NT	Double	(All pass)

When the expert doubles in this particular auction, his partner automatically leads his shortest major. One defender was in a dilemma during the Fall '95 North American Championships when his partner doubled a similar auction. He had two small in both majors - but guessed right! Absent the double, any other lead would have given the declarer the contract.

A frequent understanding, in the case of *suit contracts,* is that double of a confidently bid *game* or *slam* calls for an unusual lead. This means the defender on lead can not lead trumps or any suit bid by either of the defenders. Generally, such doubles suggest a void and it is up to partner to find it. For example, at the same Fall '95 North American Championships, sitting North would you bid 7 spades or risk a double with:

North
♠ J1082
♥ 10
♦ —
♣ QJ1098743

West
♠ 964
♥ K5
♦ AKJ94
♣ AK2

East
♠ —
♥ AQJ97632
♦ Q10865
♣ —

South
♠ AKQ753
♥ 84
♦ 732
♣ 65

West	North	East	South
	Pass[1]	4♣[2]	Pass
4♦[3]	5♣	6♥	6♠
Pass	Pass	7♦	Pass
7♥	?		

[1]Too many spades to preempt
[2]Namyats, game in hand in hearts
[3]Diamond suit with heart support

The actual North doubled, since the partnership had a firm agreement that the double asked for an unusual lead. North/South had bid both black suits, so South led the ♦7, for down one and a near top.

FIVE-LEVEL DOUBLES

The issue at the five level is quite different. The hand, instead, belongs to you and the opponents are sacrificing. Will you score better if you go on to the five level or do you stop and double the opponents? A lot of matchpoints have been lost on this decision. A well-known expert has made the following expression famous:

> **"The five level belongs to the opponents."**
> **- Grant Baze**

Experts have devised their own individual methodology for handling five-level decisions. Here is one that works.

How Partners Can Handle the Five-Level Decision When It Is Clearly Their Hand

Your Position	Passing	Bidding On	Doubling
Second hand	Shows interest in the five level - a forcing pass situation	Shows extra values, not previously shown	Shows: - Minimum values and/or - Defensive values in opponents' suit
Fourth hand (partner has already passed or doubled)	Shows agreement with partner's double	Shows near slam values or highly distributional hand	Shows not enough values to accept partner's invitation to five level

Figure 6-2

In the above partnership arrangement, there are several factors at work. Most important of all, it is a partnership decision with inputs from both sides. Note that partner's second hand double is reversible and represents just an input to the final decision. Obviously, combining the information from both hands improves the decision-making process. The tendency is not to go to the five level unless you really have a good reason - extra values that you **haven't yet shown** or **unusual distribution**.

- - - - - -

Now, you must put everything you have learned about matchpoints on hold! In the next chapter we are going to enter a new world of team events and rubber bridge. A different mind set will be necessary - get ready to ride a different horse! But first, pass your doubles quiz, if you can.

The answers to these problems begin on page 170. A lot of matchpoints are at stake during contested auctions and doubled contracts. Are you up to it?

1. | Vul: East/West |

South
♠J9864
♥3
♦A962
♣QJ7

West	North	East	South
	1♥	Pass	1♠
Pass	1NT	Pass	Pass
2♦	Pass	Pass	?

Your bid?

2. | Vul: Both |

South
♠Q105
♥6
♦Q964
♣AKJ83

West	North	East	South
		1♠	2♣
Pass	Pass	2♦	Pass
Pass	2♥	3♦	?

Your bid?

3.

Vul: None		

South
♠AJ1084
♥43
♦53
♣Q1083

West	North	East	South
Pass	1♥	Pass	1♠
1NT[1]	Pass[2]	2♣	?

[1]Sandwich NT - weak distributional takeout
[2]Partner's pass denies 3 spades (support double)

Your bid?

4.

Vul: North/South		

West
♠KJ94
♥AK7
♦J107
♣QJ10

West	North	East	South
			1♠
Pass	2♠	Pass	4♠
?			

Assess your trick-taking power - do you double or pass?

5.

| Contract: 3NT(DBL) |
| Vul: Both |

West

♠106
♥732
♦J10832
♣1076

West	North	East	South
			1♣
Pass	1♠	Pass	2NT
Pass	3NT	Double	(All pass)

Sitting West, what is your opening lead?

6.

| Vul: North/South |

South

♠KQ732
♥42
♦A875
♣AQ

West	North	East	South
			1♠
Pass	3♦[1]	3♥	4♠
5♥	Pass	Pass	?

[1]Bergen raise (4 trumps, limit raise)

The opponents are sacrificing at the five level. North passes - what should you do?

7.

Vul: North/South

South
♠742
♥AJ1075
♦ —
♣AQJ64

West	North	East	South
			1♥
2♦	3♦	5♦	?

Your bid?

8.

Contract: 6♠(DBL) Lead: ? Vul: North/South

South
♠ —
♥J98762
♦J5
♣KQ543

West	North	East	South
	3♦	3♠	Pass
4NT	Pass	5♦	Pass
6♠	Double	(All pass)	

Your lead?

ANSWERS TO CHAPTER 6 QUIZ

1. | Vul: East/West |

South
♠J9864
♥3
♦A962
♣QJ7

West	North	East	South
	1♥	Pass	1♠
Pass	1NT	Pass	Pass
2♦	Pass	Pass	?

Your bid?

The opponents are vulnerable and have come in with an "unsafe" suit (see page 15). Double and make them pay. Partner has opened the bidding and you are short in each other's suits - a big plus for defensive tricks.

2. | Vul: Both |

South
♠Q105
♥6
♦Q964
♣AKJ83

West	North	East	South
		1♠	2♣
Pass	Pass	2♦	Pass
Pass	2♥	3♦	?

Your bid?

Double. Partner obviously doesn't like your clubs and you don't like his hearts - a great misfit. You both have some defense (partner did bid vulnerable). So, go for it - the "Magic 200" and a top board!

3. | Vul: None |

South
♠AJ1084
♥43
♦53
♣Q1083

West	North	East	South
Pass	1♥	Pass	1♠
1NT[1]	Pass[2]	2♣	?

[1]Sandwich NT - weak distributional takeout
[2]Partner's pass denies 3 spades (support double)

Your bid?

Double. Your partner opened the bidding. The opponents have walked into your misfit auction with an "unsafe" suit (see page 15). Double and don't worry about West's other suit (diamonds) - partner has them. Teach the opponents a lesson.

4.

North
♠ Q106
♥ 109432
♦ Q4
♣ K84

West
♠ KJ94
♥ AK7
♦ J107
♣ QJ10

East
♠ 5
♥ Q865
♦ 532
♣ 97532

South
♠ A8732
♥ J
♦ AK986
♣ A6

West	North	East	South
			1♠
Pass	2♠	Pass	4♠
?			

Assess your trick-taking power - do you double or pass?

Doubling confidently bid game contracts usually doesn't pay off, even with 15 points and good trumps! Declarer will ruff your second heart and take out one round of trumps, finessing the trump 10. Then he will lead diamonds until you ruff. The dummy is ready to overruff you unless you play your king. Declarer will make an overtrick for a top board. By the way, if this were a team game (next chapter), an expert would have redoubled and scored a big swing!

5.

Contract: 3NT(DBL)
Vul: Both

North
♠K854
♥J95
♦K97
♣Q93

West
♠106
♥732
♦J10832
♣1076

East
♠AQJ97
♥1084
♦54
♣A52

South
♠32
♥AKQ6
♦AQ6
♣KJ84

West	North	East	South
			1♣
Pass	1♠	Pass	2NT
Pass	3NT	Double	(All pass)

Sitting West, what is your lead?

Lead the ♠10. Partner's double of 3NT is conventional and demands the lead of dummy's first bid suit. Notice that with any other lead, declarer can roll 10 or 11 tricks.

6. | Vul: North/South |

North
♠AJ98
♥63
♦KJ64
♣J74

West
♠104
♥Q109
♦32
♣1098653

East
♠65
♥AKJ875
♦Q109
♣K2

South
♠KQ732
♥42
♦A875
♣AQ

West	North	East	South
			1♠
Pass	3♦¹	3♥	4♠
5♥	Pass	Pass	?

¹Bergen raise (4 trumps, limit raise)

The opponents are sacrificing at the five level. North passes - what should you do?

Double the opponents. North has 11 points in support of spades and no wasted values in hearts. So, he passed, showing a willingness to play at the five level. You should double and not take the push for 3 reasons: (1) you do not have extra values over and *above your previous bids*; (2) you have a fairly *balanced hand* (including a doubleton in their bid suit) as opposed to unusual distribution; and (3) under such circumstances "*the 5 level belongs to the opponents.*"

7.

Vul: North/South

North
♠AQJ8
♥KQ98
♦92
♣1093

West
♠63
♥32
♦AQJ1075
♣K52

East
♠K1095
♥64
♦K8643
♣87

South
♠742
♥AJ1075
♦ —
♣AQJ64

West	North	East	South
			1♥
2♦	3♦	5♦	?

Your bid?

Bid 5 hearts. Good fitting hands with extreme distribution are worth the 5-level risk. The opponents are not vulnerable and in all probability they will go down less than your vulnerable game.

8.

Contract: 6♠(DBL)
Lead: ?
Vul: North/South

South
♠ —
♥ J98762
♦ J5
♣ KQ543

West	North	East	South
	3♦	3♠	Pass
4NT	Pass	5♦	Pass
6♠	Double	(All pass)	

Your lead?

Lead the ♥2, your longest of the unbid suits. Your partner says he can beat the hand if you do not lead his suit (diamonds) or a trump. His double calls for an unusual lead. It suggests a void in either hearts or clubs. In all likelihood it is hearts - your longest suit. You select your lowest heart as a suit-preference card to show values in clubs.

The full deal:

North
♠ 765
♥ —
♦ AK109876
♣ 1086

West
♠ K943
♥ AQ104
♦ 2
♣ AJ97

East
♠ AQJ1082
♥ K53
♦ Q43
♣ 2

South
♠ —
♥ J98762
♦ J5
♣ KQ543

Chapter 7

HOW EXPERTS WIN TEAM EVENTS *
(AND RUBBER BRIDGE)

The amazing thing about team events is that you can win or lose them before the first shot is fired - before the first match begins or the first card is played. To a large extent, success depends on whether (1) you have put together a reasonable team and (2) your team is able to handle the significant differences (in every aspect of the game) between team and matchpoint events.

Team events are a different ball game. Your approach, your strategy must be different. A new mindset is absolutely necessary. The differences in bidding and play are compelling. In teams, the goals are more straightforward - to make your contracts and defeat theirs. Your making or failing to make an extra trick or holding opponents to a minimum number of tricks is all-important in matchpoints but has virtually no weight in teams.

Why is this? The underlying reason is the difference in scoring. Matchpoint scores are based on *who does better*, no matter how slight the difference is. In teams, scoring is based on *how much better* one team does against one other team. Your only concern is with your immediate opponents, not *other* teams, playing *other* hands, at *other* tables.

To scale down the rewards and punishments so that one huge swing does not determine the outcome of the entire match, teams are scored

---

*This chapter does not specifically cover either Board-a-Match or Knockout Teams. However, the approach to Board-a-Match is similar to matchpoints discussed in earlier chapters. The approach to Knockouts is similar to Swiss Teams (and rubber bridge) discussed throughout this chapter. However, because Knockout matches are much longer, there is less luck involved and the stronger team will likely prevail. Further, as winning is the only prize in Knockouts, the state of the match near the end is likely to influence how aggressive the players are.

on an International Matchpoint Scale, commonly referred to as IMPs. The difference in scoring method and absence of a field invite risk taking and big swings. All this, in turn, generates many differences in how experts operate in the team environment. To best illustrate these differences, we are going to contrast the two forms of bridge, first as to their general considerations and then as to their bidding, play and defense.

GENERAL CONSIDERATIONS

As we have said, oddly enough you can win or lose team events before the first hand is played. Figure 7-1 displays some of the reasons why.

General Considerations Peculiar to Team Events

GENERAL CONSIDERATION	MATCHPOINT EVENTS	TEAM EVENTS
1. Practiced partnerships as teammates	N/A	Essential
2. Team approach	N/A	Trust teammates when disaster hits.
3. Careless mistakes	Can tolerate a few	Difficult to overcome, if careless mistakes create large swings
4. Team tactics	N/A	Vary tactics with caliber of opponents.
5. Safety and caution	Only in ideal contracts	Crucial in all contracts

Figure 7-1

Practiced Partnerships Are Essential

Probably, the most important consideration in winning team events is having **practiced partnerships** as teammates who at the same time will take a **team approach** to the game. There is nothing worse than returning to your teammates after a match is over to find that they have had several "accidents" (misunderstandings) - for example, missing makeable games or slams or allowing the opponents to make unmakeable ones.

To make things worse, your teammates may have felt they were losing the match due to their misunderstandings and so they took ill-conceived chances to recover the lost ground, rather than trust their partners to play well. However, in spite of your teammates' misunderstandings, you and your partner played well enough to win the match, if only your teammates had not lost their heads. The absence of a practiced partnership and a team approach can destroy any chance you may have of winning a team event.

This does not mean that you need a couple of super stars as teammates. Rather, a real partnership is needed - two people who have played together a lot, who can defend well together and who will get to most of their games and slams. Steadiness is more important than brilliance.

Careless Mistakes Can Be Your Downfall

Assuming that you have put together a reasonable team, the next best thing you can do to win is to avoid careless mistakes. In matchpoints, it is "just one board;" in teams the entire match may be at stake. Careless mistakes are due to many factors - loss of concentration, fatigue, inability to get on to the next hand (after a disaster or triumph), etc. The important thing is to be aware of this common failure and guard against it as the experts do by (1) conserving energy, (2) carefully working out what's going on at the table, (3) being especially cautious when large swings are possible and (4) trusting your teammates. For example, experts do not let a poor result distract them. The same thing may have happened at the other table. They keep their focus on the hand they are playing now.

Skill Level of Opponents Influences Tactics

At the very outset of the match, experts will judge the quality of their opponents. (Yes! They do this to you automatically and you don't even know it!) If they think the opponents skill level is appreciably below their own, they will bid moderately. Why be in a thin game and go down when your opponents are in a partscore contract? Or, why be in a pushy slam when the opponents will merely reach game? On the other hand, if they believe their opponents' skill level is equal or possibly superior to their own, experts will carefully disrupt their opponents' bidding machinery and get to all their own games and slams because they know opponents at the other table will be there.

Safety Becomes a Major Issue

Finally, safety transcends every part of the game in teams. The consequences of game, slam or even partscore swings are just too great to bear in total team scoring. As will be seen, experts take special care to reach the most secure contract and to play the hand as safely as possible.

BIDDING DIFFERENCES IN TEAM EVENTS

As can be seen in Figure 7-2, there really are extensive differences in the bidding between matchpoint and team events.

Differences in Bidding

DIFFERENCE	MATCHPOINT EVENTS	TEAM EVENTS
1. Contract type	NT first, majors next, minors last	All types **equal**; seek most comfortable, makeable contract.
2. Partscores	Fiercely fought over	Battles continue but are toned down **when vulnerable**.
3. Games/slams	Bid moderately	Aggressively bid, especially **when vulnerable**
4. Preemptive actions	A widely used tactic	**Emphasized**; can create large swings
5. Sacrificing	Aggressively pursued	Need a clear cut save; absolutely **no phantom saves**.
6. Penalties	Usually lots of leeway and only one board involved	**Bidding sounder** (especially red against white) to avoid large penalties
7. Distributional hands	Normal treatment	Insure against big swings - **bid one more** in competitive auctions.
8. Doubling	Extensive, especially at partscore levels	**More limited**; needs to be clearly your hand, a trump stack or misfit
9. Use of undiscussed conventions, treatments	Can happen infrequently	**Avoided like the plague!**

Figure 7-2

Contract Type - Find Yourself a Safe Haven

Because of scoring differences, the high stature normally accorded notrump and major suit contracts in matchpoints is now downgraded in teams to equal status with minor suits. The objective in teams is to find the most comfortable and secure contract possible. The experts simply do not risk a game or even a partscore for a slight edge in the scoring.

Vulnerability Looms Large in Teams

Vulnerability also takes on a new perspective in teams. The threat of a minus 500, 800 or 1100 looms big in teams - a real disaster, especially if the opponents do not even have a game. While partscore battles continue to be an important factor, they are not as fiercely fought over when vulnerability raises its ugly head. For example, experts will give up the fight when they feel they can defeat the opponents - how much you go plus is usually not all that important in teams as long as you go plus.

Get to Your Vulnerable Games and Slams

The very large bonuses associated with vulnerable games and slams make these contracts very attractive in team events. Experts tend to bid any game or slam which has a reasonable prospect of success. In matchpoints, the tendency is *not* to push for games and slams. In teams the tendency is just the opposite when the large bonuses are available. To illustrate, you are vulnerable and your right-hand opponent opens 2H, weak. What do you do with this hand?

♠K7
♥J94
♦AQ94
♣AK98

In the Bridge World's Master Solvers' forum, 14 experts voted for 2NT, with no clear heart stopper! Aggressiveness knows almost no bounds where a vulnerable bonus is at stake.

To illustrate, again, the bidding below has already reached 5D and you have yet to make your first bid. You hold:

♠A1032
♥10
♦AK
♣AKQJ62

West	North	East	South
2♦[1]	2♥	5♦	?

[1]Weak

In the same expert Master Solvers' forum, 16 experts bid 7C although partner had merely made an overcall. Some experts made the bid on the grounds that the opponents would have to guess whether to sacrifice. If the opponents did sacrifice, others said they would even pass the sacrifice, showing a willingness to play 7NT.

Let there be no doubt; in team events experts do not miss large game and slam bonuses - and for good reason.

Preempting Becomes an Even More Powerful Tactic

Preempting is done even more so in teams. The idea is to take space and cloud the bidding so that the opponents will not reach either their proper strain or level. Unless the vulnerability is unfavorable, an expert may even preempt 3D with hands along the following lines:

♠2
♥743
♦QJ1096
♣KJ42

Expert thinking about preempts has changed over the years. For example, in the Bridge World's Master Solvers' forum, 11 experts voted in favor of a 2H opening bid with this two-suited hand.

♠108
♥AK8532
♦J10732
♣ —

Some even volunteered that they would bid **again** (their second suit) on **their own**, if they got a chance!

Why do experts make such bids? They do so simply because it disrupts communication between the opponents to such an extent that their chances of reaching the right contract level or strain is nearly impossible or greatly reduced. This is especially true against inexperienced partnerships or inexperienced players. Preempting can also tempt the very best of opponents to bid too optimistically or to enter the bidding at too high a level. Preemptor's partner is then in a position to impose a severe penalty on the opponents. On the flip side of the coin, when team skills are fairly equal, the loss of a game or slam due to preemptive action can swing the entire match.

Sacrificing Limited to Clear Savings

Sacrificing, on the other hand, is toned down in teams to make sure that (1) the amount of savings involved is enough to justify the risk taken and (2) a penalty is not suffered when the opponents can not even make their own contract (a **phantom** save). An illustration of a clear cut save is one taken by the winners of the Vanderbilt Teams at the Spring '96 North American Bridge Championships.

North - Zia

♠AKQ982
♥105
♦KQ1094
♣ —

South - Rosenberg

♠J1064
♥32
♦J8652
♣J4

West	North	East	South
2♣[1]	4♠	6♣	6♠
Pass	Pass	Double	(All pass)

[1]Intermediate

The auction is typical of those at the expert level - leaving little room for the opponents to exchange information. Having no defense against six clubs, Rosenberg went on to sacrifice at six spades. Zia went down three for minus 500.

The save cut their loss almost in half - well worth the risk. However, at the other table, Zia's teammates suffered a major accident (7NT doubled, minus 1700!). One of the real tests of a sound partnership is the ability to weather such a disaster and continue a high level of play. Zia's team did recover, went on to the finals, and defeated Nick Nickell's "Dream Team" (Meckstroth, Rodwell, Hamman, Wolff and Freeman).

Don't Swing with Distributional Hands

The exception to this conservative approach on saves is highly distributional or wild hands where it is difficult to determine (1) whose hand it really is and (2) whether you can actually defeat the opponents at their contract. The penalty is severe if you make the wrong decision. Therefore, experts will take out an insurance policy and bid one more rather than risk a big game or slam swing. Further, such insurance precludes the deadly double swing - when the opponents' teammates can also make a game or slam but with **your cards**! To illustrate, what do you do, as South, after the opponents reach 6S on this wild auction?

Vul: Both	South
	♠98
	♥KQJ1032
	♦ —
	♣AKQ106

West	North	East	South
	Pass	1♦	4♥
4♠	Pass	6♠	?

It turns out that partner has three little trumps for you and only one spade. So, you can make 5H. But, your opponents can make 6S unless an unusual lead is made because one of them has a stiff club. Rather than depending on partner to make the perfect opening lead, many experts will hedge their bets and bid either 7C or 7H. Otherwise, something like this could happen to you.

- Small slam by opponents at your table   -1430
- 6H doubled at the other table (with your cards)   +200
                                                                  -1230

Now look at what happens when your team takes out insurance and bids one more.

- Two-trick penalty at your 7H contract   -500
- Small slam by your teammates at the other table   +1430
                                                                  +930

The difference between these two results of over 2100 points illustrates the difficulty of predicting outcomes on wildly distributional hands. If you want to insure against suffering a real calamity on wild hands in team games, bid one more.

Penalty Doubles Are More Conservative in Teams

Doubling of partscore contracts is very difficult in teams because of the inherent danger of a game swing. Total-point team scoring simply can not tolerate converting a small partscore into a game bonus. Normally, there has to be one or more of these circumstances present before an expert will double a partscore contract:

- A solid trump stack
- Misfit with partner
- Clearly the hand belongs to you and the opponents are trying to steal

When the hand does **not** belong to you, experts prefer to use the penalty double at higher levels only when they want a special lead. A double that fosters the **right lead** at the **right time** will create the opportunity for a game or slam swing for you and perhaps win the match. A further discussion of these specialized doubles can be found on page 161.

Keep Partnership Misunderstandings to an Absolute Minimum

Finally, creativity in the bidding process during a team event is not recommended. An unsuspecting partner never likes to learn about a new convention in the middle of an auction, especially in teams. Undiscussed treatments and conventions are to be avoided at all costs. An expert realizes full well that he can not afford an accident that creates (1) a swing for their opponents and (2) a loss in morale and confidence of both partner and teammates.

How Bidding Can Change the Outcome of a Match

To sum up team bidding, there are several ways you can make a real difference in the outcome of a match:

- Compete for partscores since sometimes they alone can decide the match. You have a little more leverage in teams because seldom will the opponents have the nerve to double you in a partscore contract. But, against good players be discrete when you are vulnerable.
- Bid your games and slams optimistically when vulnerable and do so **consistently**.
- Whenever possible disrupt the opponents' bidding machinery.
- Take out insurance on highly distributional hands - **bid one more**.

- Be especially alert to penalizing opponents when they are vulnerable and to lead-direction doubles that can defeat important contracts.

DECLARER PLAY DIFFERENCES IN TEAM EVENTS

Although fewer in numbers, the most dramatic differences between teams and matchpoints lies in declarer play (see Figure 7-3.)

Differences in Play of the Hand

DIFFERENCE	MATCHPOINT EVENTS	TEAM EVENTS
1. Analysis at trick one	Where are the overtricks?	What can go wrong?
2. Safety plays	Only if ideal contract	Commonly used; always secure contract first.
3. Risk taking	When odds favor; even if it jeopardizes contract	Never jeopardize the contract.

Figure 7-3

The primary objective of declarer play in teams is radically different than in matchpoints. Instead of asking what can go right, the declarer in a team event must ask *what can go wrong*? The objective at all times is to protect the contract first, then worry about overtricks. The extra benefit of an overtrick or two is never worth risking the contract. Some classic examples follow.

Illustration Number 1

Contract: 6S
Lead: ♣4

Dummy
♠A964
♥AQJ7
♦1083
♣72

♠KJ85
♥K52
♦AK7
♣AK6

The tendency in matchpoints is to play for the five missing trumps to split 3-2. Usually, declarer will start with the ace and lead up to the KJ. In teams, the expert will do just the reverse - lead the king first and then up toward the A9. This way you can handle a 4-1 split on either side and hold the trump loss to a maximum of one trick, no matter how badly they split. The expert makes these kinds of decisions by first visualizing a **bad break** in the suit and then deciding whether he can do anything about it.

Illustration Number 2

A less obvious case of a safety play (that is essential in team play) is the 6NT contract below:

```
┌─────────────────────┐        Dummy
│ Contract: 6NT       │        ♠8654
│ Lead:  ♥3           │        ♥7542
└─────────────────────┘        ♦A7
                               ♣A43


                               ♠AK
                               ♥AQ6
                               ♦KQ9842
                               ♣KQ
```

The average player will unblock the clubs, start the diamond suit by leading up to the ace and then cash the ♣A. He will be terribly embarrassed when the diamonds break 4-1 and the defender who has the fourth diamond cashes another club trick or two. This is how team matches are lost.

The expert will first count his tricks and realize that only 5 diamond tricks are necessary to make his contract. Therefore, he will unblock the ♣K and Q and play a small diamond from each hand to guard against a 4-1 split. His reward will be the small slam contract and possibly a big swing. The expert counts his tricks, looks for what can possibly go wrong and then guides his declarer play accordingly.

Illustration Number 3

On this next hand many of the matchpoint-oriented declarers would go for all 13 tricks but the team-oriented declarer realizes that he is required to give up a trick to ensure his small slam.

```
┌─────────────────────────┐
│ Contract: 6S            │
│ Lead: ♣Q                │
└─────────────────────────┘
```

Dummy
♠Q52
♥954
♦KQJ982
♣A

♠AK873
♥A2
♦A3
♣10953

After taking the opening lead with the ♣A, the expert will play the ♠Q and then a small spade, ducking it to the defenders. This leaves a trump in the dummy to stop the opponents from cashing club tricks in the event of a bad (4-1) trump break. The contract in teams is sacred. Giving up a trick to safeguard it is: "Taking care of business." The full deal:

North
♠Q52
♥954
♦KQJ982
♣A

West
♠6
♥Q108763
♦64
♣QJ82

East
♠J1094
♥KJ
♦1075
♣K764

South
♠AK873
♥A2
♦A3
♣10953

The one exception to this cautious, trick counting approach to team declarer play is the situation in which the declarer finds himself in an overly ambitious contract. In that case, he plays all out, relying on a favorable lie of the cards to make the contract.

DEFENSIVE DIFFERENCES IN TEAM EVENTS

As explained in Chapter 4, defense is by far the most difficult part of the game. In teams, experts spend a great deal of time and effort on defense. Team events are timed, however, and slow play can cause you to forfeit a board. Consequently, experts will quickly claim on hands that they play (even giving up a potential overtrick) just to have more time on another hand for defense. Why do experts give all this attention to defense? Because they do not want to give their opponents a cheap game, a cheap slam, or even an easy partscore swing. They make their opponents work for everything they get. They know excellent partnership defense is one of the very best ways to win team events.

As shown in Figure 7-4, defending in team events has an entirely different objective than in matchpoint events.

Differences in Defense

DIFFERENCE	MATCHPOINT EVENTS	TEAM EVENTS
1. Primary objective	Score the maximum possible tricks on defense.	Just defeat the contract.
2. Opening leads	Passive, unless there is a reason to go active	Take any risks to defeat contract.
3. Extra tricks by declarer	Guard against overtricks constantly.	Not crucial
4. Assume key card in partner's hand	Not done	Justified, if contract can be defeated by that assumption
5. The setting trick	Defer taking, if potential for more	Take it at earliest opportunity!

Figure 7-4

Primary Objective is to Defeat the Contract

In team events, the overriding objective in defense is to defeat the contract at any cost - a far cry from matchpoints. The expert is actively seeking any way possible to defeat a contract, even at the expense of several overtricks. Killing leads or timely shifts at trick one are at a premium. Therefore, the major change for the defender in teams is to try anything that might wreck the declarer's best laid plans. Here, acts of courage and desperation both can be rewarded. Some illustrations follow.

Illustration Number 1

```
Contract: 6S
Lead: ?
```

West
♠642
♥AKQ9763
♦ —
♣J62

West	North	East	South
1♥	Double	4♥	4♠
Pass	6♠	(All pass)	

In teams, you must lead the ♥9, hoping partner will have the jack, since he raised and will (upon reflection) get your message and return the higher ranking of the two remaining suits - a diamond. While this same lead could have been made in matchpoints, the much higher reward in teams tends to inspire such leads more often.

Illustration Number 2

Contract: 3NT	**North**
Lead: ♣K	♠ J2

North
♠ J2
♥ 1084
♦ A5
♣ Q109853

West
♠ 7
♥ Q973
♦ K1093
♣ AK74

West	**North**	**East**	**South**
			1NT
Pass	3NT	(All pass)	

Not knowing which suit to lead, West tries the ♣K to take a look at dummy and get partner's response. He soon discovers that desperate measures are needed to put the dummy out of commission. West must then lay down (sacrifice) the ♦K and destroy any hopes declarer has to establish the club suit. If this play costs a trick, the consequence in a team event is far less serious than in a matchpoint event.

Illustration Number 3

Contract: 3NT
Lead: ♥J

North
♠A10
♥Q54
♦A98632
♣A5

East
♠K62
♥K973
♦K104
♣1064

West	North	East	South
		Pass	1♠
Pass	2♦	Pass	2NT
Pass	3NT	(All pass)	

Your partner leads the ♥J, declarer ducks, you encourage with the 7 and declarer's ace wins the trick. Declarer then runs his ♦7 to your 10. What is your next play?

World class player, Eric Rodwell, laid down the ♠K, realizing that declarer's diamond suit eventually would produce the needed tricks for 3NT and that an entry was needed in partner's hand to lead hearts again. His partner, Marty Bergen, did have the ♠Q and the contract was defeated. He made the spade play in spite of South's earlier spade bid. In teams, it is worth going against the odds and placing a key card in partner's hand in order to defeat a contract.

Always Take the Setting Trick

In teams, the rule is to *"always" take the setting trick*. The tendency is to take the setting trick even at the expense of additional trick(s). Otherwise, a good declarer may find a way to make the contract, such as by squeezing one or both defenders. There is nothing more embarrassing in team events, than to forego taking the setting trick in a game contract and then watch that trick slowly disappear.

A FINAL COMMENT - KNOW WHEN TO BE AGGRESSIVE AND WHEN TO BE CONSERVATIVE

One thing transcends the entire team environment - knowing when and when not to be aggressive. Aggressiveness pays off handsomely in consistently going after vulnerable games and slams and in taking risks to defeat contracts. Further, when the conditions are right, aggressive penalty doubles can turn a match around.

On the other hand, caution is needed in finding the most comfortable contract and in safeguarding that contract in the play of the hand. Caution is needed also on distributional hands that can produce wild results. In these situations it generally pays to hedge your bets and take out insurance that all may not be as well as it may seem.

When you can judge instinctively the right times to be aggressive or conservative in team decisions, you are well on your way to becoming an expert in that arena.

- - - - - -

Now that you know much of what it takes to win team events; how about your favorite partners? Are they on the same wavelength with you? (Should you treat them to a copy of this book?) The next chapter will explore the whole issue of developing good partnerships - the very backbone of your game.

The answers to these problems begin on page 208. If you get more than 10 correct, expect to find yourself periodically on the leader board in team events. If you get as many as 15 correct, expect to be leading these events. If you get all 18 correct, consider yourself "World Class."

1.

South

♠K976
♥A5
♦4
♣AKQJ64

West	North	East	South
		Pass	1♣
Pass	1♦	Pass	1♠
Pass	4♠	Pass	?

Your bid?

2. | Vul: East/West |

South

♠86
♥J98654
♦J86
♣Q5

West	North	East	South
	2♥	Double	?

Your bid?

3. | **Vul: North/South**

South
♠AKQ753
♥KQ5
♦62
♣83

West	North	East	South
			1♠
Pass	2♥[1]	Pass	3♥
Pass	4♣	Pass	4♠
Pass	5♦	Pass	?

[1]Game forcing

Your bid?

4. | **Vul: Both**

South
♠ —
♥Q10975
♦AQ10964
♣A5

West	North	East	South
		1♠	2♠[1]
3♠	4♥	4♠	?

[1]Michaels

Your bid?

5.

Contract: 3NT
Lead: ♠9

North
♠AK4
♥64
♦AQ1094
♣A32

South
♠QJ10
♥K3
♦8765
♣KQJ4

West	North	East	South
		2♥	Pass
Pass	3♥	Pass	3NT
(All pass)			

Instead of leading his partner's suit, West lays down the ♠9. How do you play this hand to give yourself the best chance?

6.

Contract: 3NT
Lead: ♠10

North
♠Q2
♥A4
♦KQ10853
♣763

South
♠K74
♥K1032
♦A9
♣AJ85

The ♠Q wins the first trick. What is your next play?

7.

East
♠ —
♥872
♦J95
♣AQJ5432

West	North	East	South
	1♣[1]	4♣	4♥
5♣	Pass[2]	Pass	Double[3]
Pass	6♣[4]	Pass	7♥
Pass	Pass	?	

[1]Precision (16+ HCP)
[2]Forces a double
[3]Forced
[4]Club void, grand slam try

You are East, playing against Larry Cohen (South) and David Berkowitz (North) in the Vanderbilt Teams at the Spring '96 North American Championships. Your 4C bid made it difficult for them but they reached 7H anyway. What is your bid?

8.

Contract: 4H
Lead: ♠ A
Switch: Low trump

North
♠J10543
♥A987
♦73
♣84

South
♠8
♥KQ1053
♦AJ4
♣AK52

West leads the ♠ A and switches to a low trump. If you play low from dummy, East follows with a small heart. What's your best chance of making this contract?

9.

Contract: 3NT
Lead: ♠ J

North
♠832
♥965
♦AK742
♣103

South
♠AQ4
♥AK3
♦Q65
♣A742

What is your plan?

10.

Contract: 4S
Lead: ♥4
Vul: North/South

North
♠J109863
♥J2
♦75
♣872

South
♠KQ7
♥K763
♦AKJ
♣AK3

West	North	East	South
			2♣
Pass	2♦	Pass	2NT
Pass	4♥[1]	Double	4♠
(All pass)			

[1]Transfer

West leads the ♥4 to East's ace and East returns the ♥Q. Plan your play.

11.

Vul: Both

South
♠—
♥AKJ107543
♦QJ104
♣2

West	North	East	South
		4♠	5♥
5♠	Pass	Pass	?

Your bid?

12.

North	
♠A106	
♥87	
♦K8742	
♣K43	

South
♠853
♥AKQ532
♦6
♣A72

After opening the ♦A, West follows with the ♦Q. What is your plan?

If you ducked the ♦Q, congratulations! East ruffs with the ♥6. What do you do now?

13.

North
♠AQJ
♥J1054
♦AQJ
♣863

South
♠84
♥AKQ62
♦1053
♣AJ4

This problem appeared in the Sheinwold/Stewart syndicated column. Declarer refused to take the opening club lead and West switched to a diamond. How do you play the hand to make 4H?

14.

Contract: 3NT
Lead: ♠7
Vul: North/South

North
♠AQ95
♥63
♦A853
♣Q104

South
♠1032
♥Q74
♦KQ
♣AKJ83

If West's ♠7 lead is his fourth best, you have 12 tricks. The overtricks are worth 3 IMPs. What is your proper play at trick one?

15.

Contract: 3NT
Lead: ♠4
Vul: Both

North
♠J75
♥A103
♦QJ10985
♣4

West
♠Q1064
♥K84
♦AK
♣Q865

West	North	East	South
			1NT[1]
Pass	3NT	(All pass)	

[1] 15-17 points

Dummy's ♠J wins the first trick. Declarer plays the ♦Q to your K. How do you proceed?

16.

Contract: 4S
Lead: ♥A
Vul: Both

North
♠AQ43
♥Q642
♦85
♣Q93

East
♠62
♥K108753
♦A7
♣752

West	North	East	South
			1NT[1]
Pass	2♣	Pass	2♠
Pass	4♠	(All pass)	

[1] 15-17 points

West opens the ♥A. After thinking about the entire hand, what line of defense do you as East adopt and in so doing, what heart do you play at trick one?

17.

Contract: 5S
Lead: ♥K

North
♠KQ6
♥932
♦AKJ109
♣84

South
♠AJ1085432
♥ —
♦642
♣K9

West	North	East	South
1♥	2♦	3♥[1]	4♠
5♥	5♠	(All pass)	

[1]Preemptive

Eddie Kantar presented this problem in the 1996 ACBL Bridge Calendar. West opens the ♥K and East encourages. You are declarer as South. What is your plan?

18.

Contract: 4H
Lead: ♠10
Vul: Both

North
♠Q632
♥A3
♦62
♣A9842

South
♠4
♥KQJ1094
♦AK753
♣7

West	North	East	South
			1♥
Pass	2♣	2♠	3♦
Pass	3NT	Pass	4♥
(All pass)			

Our last problem is also from the Sheinwold/Stewart syndicated bridge columnn. East overtakes the ♠10 lead with the jack and continues the spade suit. You ruff the second round. How do you expect to make the contract?

ANSWERS TO CHAPTER 7 QUIZ

1.

North
♠ 10832
♥ KQ7
♦ AKQ6
♣ 32

South
♠ K976
♥ A5
♦ 4
♣ AKQJ64

West	North	East	South
		Pass	1♣
Pass	1♦	Pass	1♠
Pass	4♠	Pass	?

Your bid?

The average player, still somewhat under the influence of matchpoint scoring, will assume South has good values in spades and wind up in 6S - down one or two. During the rest of the match, he will worry about what happened at the other table. After using Blackwood, the expert will be content to play in a safe and secure contract of 6C, even if it costs a few IMPs.

2.

Vul: East/West

South
- ♠86
- ♥J98654
- ♦J86
- ♣Q5

West	North	East	South
	2♥	Double	?

Your bid?

One of your opponents likely has a heart void. If so, your side either has no defensive tricks or at most one. The expert bid here is to throw a monkey wrench into the opponents' bidding machine. In a Bridge World Master Solvers' forum, experts were split almost evenly between a jump to 5, 6 and 7 hearts with 5 hearts receiving a slight edge. Consider yourself correct if you chose any one of those bids.

3.　| Vul: North/South |　South

♠AKQ753
♥KQ5
♦62
♣83

West	North	East	South
			1♠
Pass	2♥¹	Pass	3♥
Pass	4♣	Pass	4♠
Pass	5♦	Pass	?

¹Game forcing

Your bid?

In a practiced partnership, bid your grand slam in hearts. You have all the controls and most probably 13 tricks. In team events, go for the vulnerable slam bonuses and do it consistently. The payoffs for those that succeed will more than offset the few that don't (except on a bad day ☹).

4. | **Vul: Both**

South
♠ —
♥Q10975
♦AQ10964
♣A5

West	North	East	South
		1♠	2♠[1]
3♠	4♥	4♠	?

[1]Michaels

Your bid?

Bid 5D. According to the Bridge World Master Solvers Forum (January, 1996), 16 experts favored the 5D bid. By showing the other Michaels suit, the expert accomplishes four things:

- He shows a strong offensive hand and a willingness to go to slam if partner has a double fit or extra values.

- He takes out insurance against a distributional hand in case the opponents can make their vulnerable 4S game.

- He shows defensive values in diamonds in case the opponents ultimately play the hand.

- He makes the final action subject to the advice and consent of both partners, not unilateral.

5.

Contract: 3NT
Lead: ♠9

North
♠AK4
♥64
♦AQ1094
♣A32

West
♠9876
♥A92
♦J32
♣1086

East
♠532
♥QJ10875
♦K
♣975

South
♠QJ10
♥K3
♦8765
♣KQJ4

West	North	East	South
		2♥	Pass
Pass	3♥	Pass	3NT
(All pass)			

Instead of leading his partner's suit, West lays down the ♠9. How do you play this hand to give yourself the best chance?

Lay down the ♦A. If East gets in he will, of course, kill you with a heart switch. This is a safety play in the event East has a singleton king. At worst, it costs only a trick but look at what you can save. In the event East has the guarded ♦K and West the ♥A, as expected, there is nothing you can do but go down gracefully.

6.

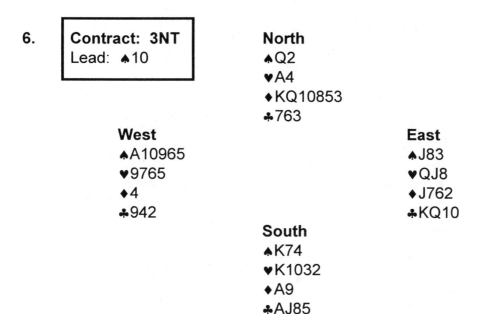

Contract: 3NT
Lead: ♠10

North
♠Q2
♥A4
♦KQ10853
♣763

West
♠A10965
♥9765
♦4
♣942

East
♠J83
♥QJ8
♦J762
♣KQ10

South
♠K74
♥K1032
♦A9
♣AJ85

The ♠Q wins the first trick. What is your next play?

After winning the ♠Q, the expert would lead a low diamond to the nine to guard against a 4-1 split and, at the same time, prevent the dangerous hand (East) from getting the lead. In teams, giving up one trick is cheap insurance indeed against the loss of a game contract.

7. | **Vul: North/South**

North
♠ AKQ9632
♥ A63
♦ AQ7
♣ —

West
♠ J8754
♥ 5
♦ 108432
♣ 97

East
♠ —
♥ 872
♦ J95
♣ AQJ5432

South
♠ 10
♥ KQJ1094
♦ K6
♣ K1086

West	North	East	South
	1♣[1]	4♣	4♥
5♣	Pass[2]	Pass	Double[3]
Pass	6♣[4]	Pass	7♥
Pass	Pass	?	

[1] Precision (16+ HCP)
[2] Forces a double
[3] Forced
[4] Club void, grand slam try

You are East, playing against Larry Cohen (South) and David Berkowitz (North) in the Vanderbilt Teams at the Spring '96 North American Championships. Your 4C bid made it difficult for them but they reached 7H anyway. What is your bid?

The actual opponent doubled for an unusual lead from his partner in the hope of defeating the contract. Unfortunately his partner had equal length in both the unbid suits (spades and diamonds) and would not have known from the bidding which suit to lead to his partner for a ruff. But, he was spared this flip of a coin decision. David, believing that the doubler wanted and would get a spade ruff, continued the bidding with 7S! The opponents doubled again and he couldn't cope with the 5-0 trump break (down one).

At the other table the opponents stopped in 6S. They took a very fine safety play, finessing the spade 10 for plus 1430 - a swing of 17 IMPs against Larry and David. Had the spades broken better, they would have won 13 IMPs - a swing of 30 IMPs - a heartbreaking disaster for two national champions.

This hand illustrates 3 important principles of team play:

- When you feel your hand justifies a grand slam bid, go for it. Due to the large bonuses involved, the element of consistency will pay off for you in team events over the long haul.

- Be a risk taker when it comes to defending against these slams; double if it might help your partner get off to the right lead.

- When playing hands, especially lucrative slam contracts, always ask yourself what can go wrong and then guard against it - huge swings are at stake.

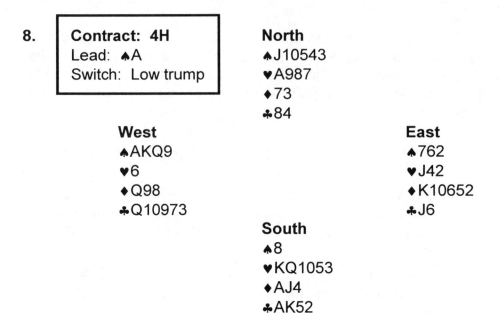

8.

Contract: 4H
Lead: ♠A
Switch: Low trump

North
♠J10543
♥A987
♦73
♣84

West
♠AKQ9
♥6
♦Q98
♣Q10973

East
♠762
♥J42
♦K10652
♣J6

South
♠8
♥KQ1053
♦AJ4
♣AK52

West leads the ♠ A and switches to a low trump. If you play low from dummy, East follows with a small heart. What's your best chance of making this contract?

Your plan of action should be based on two time-honored team principles; first, count your tricks and second, ask yourself, "What can go wrong?" Take the trump trick in dummy (East's best defense is to duck). Then, lead a diamond to your Jack and West's Queen. Take any return and trump a diamond low in dummy. Next, cash your two top clubs and trump a club with your ♥A! Otherwise, East will defeat the contract by overruffing and taking out your last trump. These are the plays that win team events.

9.

Contract: 3NT
Lead: ♠ J

North
♠832
♥965
♦AK742
♣103

South
♠AQ4
♥AK3
♦Q65
♣A742

What is your plan?

In teams, the expert will attempt to secure this contract by ducking a diamond. This ensures nine tricks and the contract provided diamonds are not 5-0. In matchpoints, he would play the odds (a 3-2 break) and risk going down if the diamond suit broke badly.

10.

Contract: 4S
Lead: ♥4
Vul: North/South

North
♠J109863
♥J2
♦75
♣872

West
♠A54
♥4
♦Q8642
♣9654

East
♠2
♥AQ10985
♦1093
♣QJ10

South
♠KQ7
♥K763
♦AKJ
♣AK3

West	North	East	South
			2♣
Pass	2♦	Pass	2NT
Pass	4♥[1]	Double	4♠
(All pass)			

[1]Transfer

West leads the ♥4 to East's ace and East returns the ♥Q. Plan your play.

You have 10 tricks, but if you went up with the ♥K, West ruffed it and your tricks are now reduced to 9. Since, in teams, ensuring the contract is first and foremost, the expert will duck the ♥Q and later on pitch his losing club on the ♥K. Again, visualizing what can possibly go wrong pays off.

11. | Vul: Both |

South
♠—
♥AKJ107543
♦QJ104
♣2

West	North	East	South
		4♠	5♥
5♠	Pass	Pass	?

Your bid?

Bid 6H, taking out insurance in case the opponents can make their vulnerable game. In wild hands, such as this, any thing can happen. For example, there is the possibility of a double swing against you:

- Your opponents make 5S at your table   -650
- Your opponents' teammates make 5H at   -650
  the other table with your cards

              Total Swing   -1300

Have you thought about the possibility that you might actually make 6H? While it may be unlikely, suppose partner has the ♦A and the ♦K is onside.

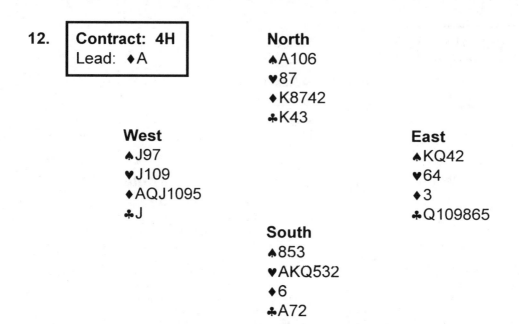

12. | **Contract: 4H** Lead: ♦A

North
♠A106
♥87
♦K8742
♣K43

West
♠J97
♥J109
♦AQJ1095
♣J

East
♠KQ42
♥64
♦3
♣Q109865

South
♠853
♥AKQ532
♦6
♣A72

After opening the ♦A, West follows with the ♦Q. What is your plan?

If you ducked the ♦Q, congratulations! East ruffs with the ♥6. What do you do now?

Pitch a loser. Your first duck of the ♦Q was a good play because East would have ruffed out your 10th trick. (Are you counting?) When East ruffs the diamond, if you overruff with an honor you will go down because a trump trick will be promoted for the opponents. Two fundamental safety plays were necessary on this hand: (1) *preserve* your ♦K until later because it is your *10th trick* and (2) pitch a loser anytime overruffing *might promote a trump trick in the opponent's hand*.

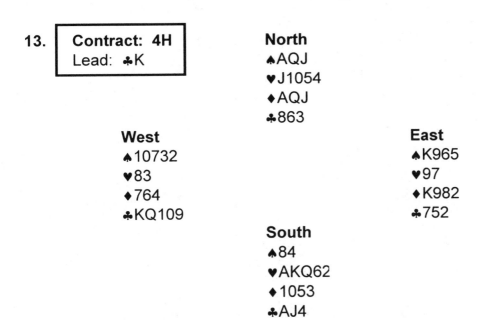

13. | Contract: 4H
Lead: ♣K

North
♠AQJ
♥J1054
♦AQJ
♣863

West
♠10732
♥83
♦764
♣KQ109

East
♠K965
♥97
♦K982
♣752

South
♠84
♥AKQ62
♦1053
♣AJ4

This problem appeared in the Sheinwold/Stewart syndicated column. Declarer refused to take the opening club lead and West switched to a diamond. How do you play the hand to make 4H?

The typical matchpoint player finesses for the ♦K, hoping that one or both of his two finesses are on. In teams, the expert shuns the possibility of an extra trick in favor of a sure thing. He goes up with the ♦A, takes out trumps and hooks the ♠K. Whether it wins or loses, he discards his losing club on the third spade and ensures his contract. He knew his plan would succeed because he counted his tricks - 5 hearts, 2 spades, 2 diamonds and 1 club.

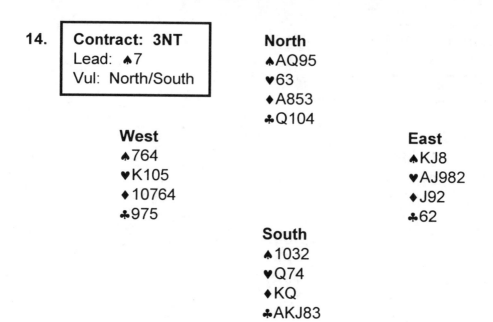

14. | **Contract: 3NT**
Lead: ♠7
Vul: North/South

North
♠AQ95
♥63
♦A853
♣Q104

West
♠764
♥K105
♦10764
♣975

East
♠KJ8
♥AJ982
♦J92
♣62

South
♠1032
♥Q74
♦KQ
♣AKJ83

If West's ♠7 lead is his fourth best, you have 12 tricks. The overtricks are worth 3 IMPs. What is your proper play at trick one?

Play the ♠A. In teams, always count your tricks first. As you have nine, you should go up with the ♠A and secure the contract first. Afterwards, you can be pleased if any overtricks come your way. The few IMPs involved are not worth the risk of going down in a cold vulnerable game. On this particular hand, if you got greedy, and ducked the opening lead, East grabbed the trick and put a low heart on the table (in a heartbeat) for down two - an 800 point swing in the match. Try to explain that one to your teammates (or pard)!

15.

Contract: 3NT
Lead: ♠4
Vul: Both

North
♠J75
♥A103
♦QJ10985
♣4

West
♠Q1064
♥K84
♦AK
♣Q865

East
♠932
♥Q962
♦743
♣1092

South
♠AK8
♥J75
♦62
♣AKJ73

West	North	East	South
			1NT[1]
Pass	3NT	(All pass)	

[1]15-17 points

Dummy's ♠J wins the first trick. Declarer plays the ♦Q to your K. How do you proceed?

Hoping that declarer has just 2 diamonds, try to wreck his plan to set up the diamond suit by leading (sacrificing) your ♥K. Declarer can try to stave off defeat by ducking, but a heart continuation will do him in. And, your teammates will be talking about your play for days! It is typical of the risks taken on defense at teams but not necessarily at matchpoints.

16.

Contract: 4S
Lead: ♥A
Vul: Both

North
♠AQ43
♥Q642
♦85
♣Q93

West
♠J108
♥A
♦J96432
♣1084

East
♠62
♥K108753
♦A7
♣752

South
♠K975
♥J9
♦KQ10
♣AKJ6

West	North	East	South
			1NT[1]
Pass	2♣	Pass	2♠
Pass	4♠	(All pass)	

[1]15-17 points

West opens the ♥A. After thinking about the entire hand, what line of defense do you as East adopt and in so doing, what heart do you play at trick one?

Partner must be the one with a singleton heart, since South opened 1NT. To collect four defensive tricks you need to promote a trump trick for partner. Therefore, play an unusually high suit preference card (the ♥10), asking for the higher ranking of the two remaining suits - diamonds. After taking your ♦A and ♥K, lead a third heart. Partner will then either overruff if declarer ruffs low or pitch off if declarer ruffs high. Either way, partner gets a trump trick and you defeat the contract - your primary objective at teams.

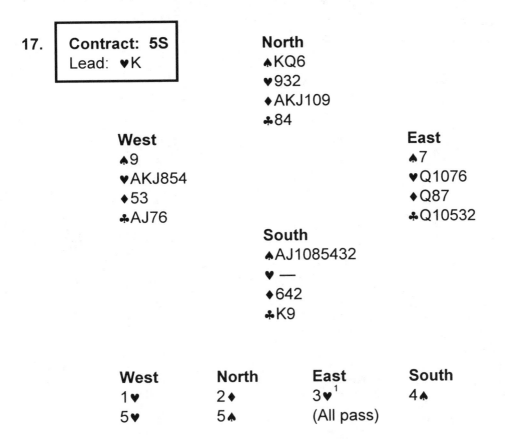

17. | Contract: 5S
Lead: ♥K

North
♠KQ6
♥932
♦AKJ109
♣84

West
♠9
♥AKJ854
♦53
♣AJ76

East
♠7
♥Q1076
♦Q87
♣Q10532

South
♠AJ1085432
♥ —
♦642
♣K9

West	North	East	South
1♥	2♦	3♥[1]	4♠
5♥	5♠	(All pass)	

[1]Preemptive

Eddie Kantar presented this problem in the 1996 ACBL Bridge Calendar. West opens the ♥K and East encourages. You are declarer as South. What is your plan?

When you ask yourself the right question (what can go wrong?), the first play is easy - pitch a diamond. Now you can set up the diamond suit without the threat of East getting in to ruin you with a club shift. In this case a little insurance pays big dividends.

Contract: 4H
Lead: ♠10
Vul: Both

North
♠Q632
♥A3
♦62
♣A9842

West
♠107
♥72
♦QJ984
♣Q1053

East
♠AKJ985
♥865
♦10
♣KJ6

South
♠4
♥KQJ1094
♦AK753
♣7

West	North	East	South
			1♥
Pass	2♣	2♠	3♦
Pass	3NT	Pass	4♥
(All pass)			

Our last problem is also from the Sheinwold/Stewart syndicated bridge columnn. East overtakes the ♠10 lead with the jack and continues the spade suit. You ruff the second round. How do you expect to make the contract?

The surest way to collect 10 tricks is to lay down the ♦A and then a small one. You now have 6 hearts, 2 diamonds, 1 club and you can ruff one diamond with the ♥A. As you can see, if you try to cash the ♦K instead, East will ruff it and you'll come up short with just 9 tricks - a swing of 720 points and some unhappy teammates!

Chapter 8

HOW TO BUILD SUCCESSFUL PARTNERSHIPS

> **"The key to good bridge is *partnership*, rather than individual skills."   - William Root**

Bill Root said it exactly right. If you are serious about advancing your bridge play and becoming a winner, there is no alternative to patiently building good partnerships. Few endeavors depend on partnership as much as bridge. Partnership in bridge is supreme. The needs and desires of the two individuals must be subordinated to what is best for the partnership. The "partnership card" is the most important one in the deck.

Bob Hamman, recognized as the best player in the world over the past decade is reputed *also* to be one of the best partners around. The connection between successful results and partnership is undeniable. Just to illustrate, two world class players failed to make the top fifteen in a major national event due to misunderstandings, disagreements and recriminations. In the same event, two less recognized players with a great partnership style went on to win the event.

A deep and abiding faith in the partnership concept is essential. Otherwise, you will not invest the time and effort required to build successful partnerships. Figure 8-1 depicts a framework for building such partnerships.

Building Successful Partnerships

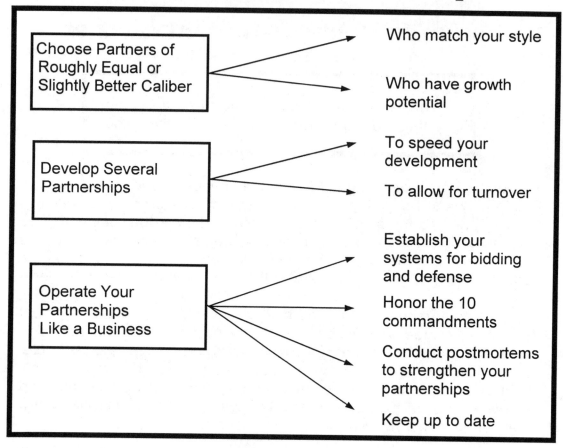

Figure 8-1

CHOOSE PARTNERS OF ROUGHLY EQUAL OR SLIGHTLY BETTER CALIBER

The preference for forming a new partnership is for the two partners to be close enough in ability to challenge each other to play better and to grow together, with neither dominating. A significant gap in ability is not a sound foundation to begin a successful partnership. It ultimately leads to domination by the stronger partner, not a cooperative, working partnership. Eventually, the stronger partner gets frustrated and takes his frustration out on the weaker one or abandons him.

There are three characteristics you need to seek out in a new partner. The first is a matching bidding style. A free lancer who "operates" is a source of great dissatisfaction to the disciplined bidder. The two types simply clash. It is better to choose partners who are compatible with your style.

The second characteristic you need in a partner is growth potential. The type of person you are seeking is someone who is flexible, open to change and able to grow at about the same pace as you are growing.

The third characteristic you would like to have in a partner is a supportive rather than combative attitude. It is a very special partner indeed who can be self-critical, acknowledge his own mistakes and even take some responsibility for yours.

DEVELOP SEVERAL PARTNERSHIPS

We all learn from our partners although we may not recognize or admit it. Each partner has different strengths which you can draw upon at various times and each partner will challenge you to play better in different ways. So having several partners will speed your development as a bridge player.

In addition, we all lose partners at one time or another. This can happen due to geographic relocation, incompatibility, or the fact that one partner simply outgrows the other. Turnover in partners is a fact of life. So, it is best to always have several ongoing partnerships. Otherwise, you are destined to suffer a major setback in your bridge game when your favorite partner abandons you for one reason or another.

OPERATE YOUR PARTNERSHIPS LIKE A BUSINESS

Your partnerships need to have a continuous program for improving and updating your systems for bidding and defense. Initially, with any new partnership, you will want to establish a bidding system, including the conventions and understandings acceptable to both partners. As time goes on new ideas and conventions can be explored and integrated into your system, if useful.

Most helpful is to practice bidding hands. Such hands can be computer generated. Many random hand generators have features for generating specific types of hands that you may be having trouble with; for example, slam hands, weak notrump hands or Flannery hands. Another excellent source of hands for bidding practice is the "Challenge the Champs" feature in the Bridge World magazine. Bidding against the experts is challenging, informative and fun.

The most important goal at the table in operating a partnership is to establish a comfortable relationship with your partner and maintain partnership confidence and morale, especially when things go wrong. If you work hard at this, you will bring out the very best in your partner. The ten commandments below will help you achieve this goal.

Maintaining Partnership Confidence and Morale

THE 10 COMMANDMENTS OF GOOD PARTNERSHIP BRIDGE

- Take immediate responsibility for individual mistakes; capitalize on them to improve your game.

- Never embarrass partner at the table.

- *Go on to the next hand,* discuss disasters later when emotions subside and perspective returns.

- Limit discussions during the game to simple clarifications.

- Consult acknowledged experts on differences of opinion; give your hand, not partner's.

- Stick to understandings reached as if they were gospel.

- Always trust partner over the opponents.

- Share key decisions with partner as opposed to making unilateral ones.

- Respect partner's judgment, don't second guess him.

- Be sensitive to partner's needs at the table and responsive to his signals.

Figure 8-2

Most of these commandments are obvious and self-explanatory, yet at times they are very difficult to honor at the table. It is amazing what the passage of time and some thought after a disaster will do for your perspective. For example, what you initially perceived to be your partner's fault, may actually turn out to be your own!

> **"It is much easier to receive (or give) constructive criticism, and analyze your poor results *without* the "ears" of the bridge community listening in."**
> **- William Root**

The bottom line is if you can manage to keep your poise and move on to the next hand gracefully, it may save your partnership and without a doubt improve your bridge results.

Consult with Partner on Key Decisions

It will pay to share key decisions (consult) with partner on important matters such as whether you should stop short of or proceed on to a game or slam. For one thing, any good partner will resent unilateral decisions (whether they tell you or not). More importantly, combining your information on the hand and using both heads rather than one will usually produce better decisions.

Play Partnership Bridge

We can not overstress the importance of playing partnership bridge at all times. Partnership bridge is when you disobey your own instincts and follow partner's direction out of respect for his judgment and the partnership as a whole. The very rare exception is when you have a great deal more information than partner has and you are nearly 100 percent confident that taking a different direction on a hand is the right thing to do. Partner will understand, but *only* if you are right! Even if your efforts to play partnership bridge turn out to be wrong once in a while, preserving partnership confidence and morale is so much more important than the result on any one particular hand.

Further, it is important to always believe in your partner's bidding. For example, after one partner did not bid what the other expected, how many times have you heard, "but the opponents bid ..." The bottom line is whatever partner has said during the auction **always has priority** over what the opponents have said - even if the opponents are experts.

Finally, you need to go out of your way to meet partner's needs at the table and make things as easy as possible for him, both in the bidding and defense. For example, have you and your partner ever protected the same suit while declarer ran away with unearned tricks in an unprotected suit? Or, have you ever set up a suit to run against a 3NT contract only to find your partner breaking communication by pitching his last card in your suit? These kind of disasters are usually preventable and should be carefully avoided if you want to have a smooth working, successful partnership.

Conduct Postmortems To Strengthen Your Partnerships

At the end of the bridge session, some players will check to see if they are among the leaders and, if not, immediately head for home. However, players desiring to progress will stick around, whether they are on the leader board or not, and take the time to record and later analyze their results. The objective is to zoom in on what you did right and what you need to work on. These kind of partnership discussions will, in turn, improve how you bid and defend hands in successive events.

In play of the hand, if you detect a pattern of misplay, you may mention a principle that might be useful to your partner. Otherwise, you should not comment on partner's declarer play.

Figure 8-3 is a guide to strengthening partnerships and resolving differences.

Strengthening Partnerships and Resolving Differences

BIDDING	DEFENSE	DECLARER PLAY
Resolve bidding problems with: • Chp. 2 - How the Experts Bid • Chp. 10 literature • Expert opinion	Resolve defensive problems with: • Chp. 4 - The Five Lines of Defense • Chp. 5 - Opening Leads • Chp. 10 literature	Strengthen declarer play with: • Chp. 10 "classics" on card play technique • Chp. 10 computer programs

Figure 8-3

When the above guidelines do not resolve partnership differences, you have two choices:

- Convince one or the other partner to change his way of thinking, or

- Take the issue up with a respected (or your favorite) expert and agree to try his way.

Keep Up to Date

Contract bridge has been ever changing since its inception some 75 years ago. Tournament bridge has accelerated these changes. Each year enlightening books are written on various aspects of the game. Further, new bidding conventions emerge periodically that need to be explored. Therefore, to reach your goals in bridge, your partnerships will need to:

- Update your convention cards based on modern conventions in regular use by the top players (see Chp. 9).

- Update your thinking based on the current literature and new developments (see Chp. 10).

Of course, our next two chapters will only be a start. To keep abreast of significant changes in the game, you will want to periodically review bridge publications for new material of interest.

Operating a Partnership Involved in a Special Relationship

The history of bridge is replete with bitter and acrimonious experiences of partnerships that either were married or had an emotional attachment. A personal relationship in bridge adds a lot more baggage to an already difficult situation. Nevertheless, there have been some successes. What seems to make the difference is (1) a wonderful relationship and (2) a desire to play together that is strong enough to **make it work**. Some written understandings may be useful as to the behavior expected from each at the table when things go wrong. For example, you may wish to enter into a contract as to how you will handle mistakes at the table, including misunderstandings and disagreements.

A book has been published in recent years on the subject of relationships in bridge, "How to Play Bridge With Your Spouse (And Survive) by Roslyn Teukolsky. It is beautifully written, enlightening and entertaining.

— — — — — —

Are you ready to test your convention card against the experts? If so, go on to the next chapter.

Chapter 9

CONVENTIONS USED BY THE TOP PLAYERS

The growth in conventions since the 1950s has revolutionized the game of bridge. Today, there are a vast number of conventions and convention cards differ, even among the experts. Bridge players, faced with innumerable possibilities, wonder what might be the ideal convention card. To help you in deciding what the optimum convention card for you might be, we offer below the **more important conventions** in **regular** use by the **top players**.

In the early days of bridge, there were no convention cards. A few simple conventions existed, such as Stayman and Blackwood, which were well understood by nearly everyone. In the 1950s some highly successful pairs started using natural bids for other purposes to solve problems they had at the table. One of the first of these new conventions was the negative double. Many additional conventions followed, some quite innovative and others of dubious worth. Eventually, this growth of conventions required the development of a special card.

In some parts of the bridge community conventions have achieved an exaggerated sense of importance. There is a preoccupation with them, especially the more exotic ones. To guard against their overuse, experts have come up with tests to determine the worth of any new convention:

- Is it effective on the hands for which it was designed? In other words, does it greatly improve your bidding?
- Does the convention compensate for the loss of the natural bid it displaces?
- Has it a reasonable frequency of occurrence?
- Is the convention worth the extra memory required? Will you remember it in the heat of battle?

Over the years, a number of conventions have met these tests. Today, typically you will find the ones below on an expert's convention card. Our criterion is simple; major or widespread use of the convention by top players across the nation. What you are ultimately seeking in your review of the expert's convention card is a collection of conventions that blend together and deal effectively with the range of hands that come up most often at the table. As we take a snapshot of each portion of that card, we will highlight a few of the conventions.

Space considerations don't permit us to discuss all of the conventions but if you want more detail, see Everyone's Guide to the New Convention Card by Marty Bergen and other literature cited in Chapter 10.

The Expert's Convention Card (Part 1)

General Approach
- 2/1 Game Force

Notrump Openings
- 1NT Ranges Used:
  — Strong (15-17)
  — Weak (12-14)
  — Mini (10-12)
- 2NT (20-21)
- Gambling 3NT
- Stayman
- Smolen
- 4-Way Transfers
- Coping With Interference Over NT
  — Negative Doubles
  — Lebensohl

Major Openings
- 5-Card Majors
- 1NT Forcing
- Limit Raises
- Bergen Raises
- Jacoby 2NT (Forcing Raise)
- Splinters
- Fit Showing Jumps
- Reverse Drury

Figure 9-1

Almost without exception top players are using the **Two-Over-One system with 5-card major openings**. There are variations in 2/1 style but the one most widely used is unconditionally forcing to 3NT or four of a suit.

As for **opening notrumps**, there is no consensus - they range from mini to weak to strong. The mini and weak notrumps, because of their preemptive values, are becoming increasingly popular. Some experts play two-way notrumps; that is, they vary in strength depending on vulnerability and position.

In contested auctions, most experts now use the Law of Total Tricks to guide the level of their auctions (see page 10). Therefore, **Bergen raises**, which distinguish between 3- and 4-card support, have become increasingly popular in recent years. For the same reason, when players overcall, their partners use special conventions - **mixed raises, high/low cues, jump raises** - to show not only relative values but also the length of their trump support.

The Expert's Convention Card (Part 2)

Minor Openings
- As short as 3; bid best minor
- Inverted Minors
- Splinters
- 2NT Response = Invitational

Opening Two Bids
- 2C Strong (Controls Response)
- 2D Weak (5-10) or Flannery (11-14)
- 2H/2S Weak (5-10)
- Ogust (Modified)

Other Conventional Calls
- New Minor Forcing
- Fourth Suit Forcing
- Weak Jump Shifts/Overcalls
- Jordan NT
- Unusual NT
- Michaels
- Sandwich NT = Takeout
- Equal Level Conversion
- Jump Cue (Mixed Raise)
- Hi/Lo Cue
- Jump Raise (Preemptive)

Figure 9-2

Wide ranging **weak 2 and 3 bids** are the current style among experts. Two bids are often 5-card suits so a modified form of **Ogust** has emerged. When used, this convention reveals whether the opener (1) has a 5- or 6-card suit and (2) is in the lower or upper range of his bid.

The **sandwich notrump** has replaced the strong notrump overcall in fourth position because it is an ideal way of showing a distributional takeout of the two unbid suits. After the opponents have bid two suits, this type of hand shows up more often than the balanced strong notrump hand.

The Expert's Convention Card (Part 3)

Special Doubles

- Negative
- Responsive
- Support
- Cooperative
- Snapdragon
- Maximal

Defenses To Conventions

- Opening NT
  — D.O.N.T.
  — Cappelletti
- Michaels
  — Unusual Over Michaels
- Unusual NT
  — Unusual Over Unusual
- Weak 2 Bids
  — Take Out Double /Lebensohl
  — Kantar (Leaping Michaels)

Figure 9-3

Much of the action at the table today is at the partscore level. This is where matchpoint and team events can be decided. To help compete during these fierce battles, the experts use the *cooperative double* and *snapdragon double*.

The *cooperative double* usually comes up at the two or three level and says to partner:

- I have some additional values.
- It may be our hand.
- My next action is unclear.
- Please do something intelligent.

This gives responder the option of passing for penalty or bidding one more depending on such things as holding in the opponents' suit, length of trump support, shape and location of values.

The **snapdragon double** (sometimes referred to as an extended responsive double) is akin to the **negative double** in that it gives the overcaller some of the same options. It says:

- I have the unbid suit(s) - (either 1 or 2).
- If there is only one unbid suit, I have tolerance for (can stand) your overcalled suit.
- I have some values (around 8 or more points) and want to compete.

The overcaller has options too; he can identify a new fit or stay with his original suit. The **snapdragon** double is a wonderful tool for competitive bidding auctions.

DEFENSIVE CONVENTIONS

In earlier times an opening strong notrump scared off the competition - not today! Among the more popular conventions used to compete with strong or weak notrumps are **D.O.N.T.** (Disturbing Opponents NoTrump) and **Cappelletti**. They offer a wide range of options for entering the bidding. These conventions not only interfere with the opponents' bidding but often offer contracts more advantageous (scorewise) than allowing the opponents to play the hand.

D.O.N.T. has several distinct advantages: (1) you can enter the auction with ease, (2) you can show all one- and two-suited hands without getting to the three level and (3) you can find a safe haven in any suit at the two level.

Experts have devised **defenses** to some conventions. For example, when the opponents promise 2 specific suits, as in the **unusual notrump** and **Michaels cue bid**, experts use the **unusual over unusual** as a counter convention. This counter convention offers cue bids of the opponents' implied suits to show strong support for either partner's opening bid or the unbid suit. If instead a double is made, a lucrative penalty situation may develop if partner is interested.

As a counter to the frequent use of weak 2 bids, some experts use **Kantar (leaping Michaels)**. To illustrate, a leap to the four level in a minor over a weak two spades bid shows that minor and hearts (the other major). Kantar has other options which can get you to a 3NT contract or a minor-suit game.

The Expert's Convention Card (Part 4)

Slam Bidding

- Cue Bidding
- Roman Key Card Blackwood
- Gerber (Jump Over Notrump)
- Grand Slam Force

Defensive Card Play

- Leads
  — Third from even, low from odd
  — Fourth best
  — Attitude
  — Zero or two higher
- Signals
  — Upside down or standard
  — Odd-even discards
  — Present count
  — Suit preference
  — Smith echo

Figure 9-4

SLAM BIDDING

The expert's preference for exploring slam contracts is *cuebidding* or in the case of wild distribution to simply blast there. In most slam bidding the central question is: "Does the partnership have the overall values and controls to warrant a slam contract?" Cuebidding helps to answer that question. For example, partner can initially refuse to cue bid and thereby show minimal values and no interest or he may show interest by cuebidding controls up the line.

This is not so in the case of the *Blackwood* or *Gerber* convention. Partner must respond and sometimes very unhappily. At the first hint of slam possibilities, some players rush to Blackwood. This is not its purpose. Rather, Blackwood was created as a device to keep people out of slam off two quick tricks. Premature use of Blackwood *robs* the partnership of the very space needed to explore whether or not slam really is a good idea. And, some Blackwood responses might get the auction too high. Experts favor the convention (in keycard form) only when a slam contract is highly likely and they merely want to see if they have the required number of keycards.

OPENING LEAD METHODS

As outlined in Chapter 4 on defense, there is considerable variety within expert circles as to lead methods. The most popular against suit contracts is third from an even number of cards and low from an odd number of cards, and against notrump contracts is either fourth best or attitude. Zero or two higher leads from such combinations as KJ10 or Q109 are in common usage. However, some experts elect to play the middle card when on opening lead in an effort to confuse declarer.

SIGNALLING METHODS

As to signalling methods, experts again differ on various ones but for *attitude* and *count* they tend to favor *upside down*. Two additional signalling methods are used by some experts to help their partners work out high cards and distribution. They use *odd-even discards* to help partner locate where their high card values are. They use present count to help partner figure out the hand's distribution. If you are not familiar with these signalling methods, the next chapter will provide you with a ready source of information.

Hopefully, this chapter has given you some insight into what your convention card should contain. Obviously, you will need to familiarize yourself with the intricacies of any new conventions you want to explore and consider how they fit into your system. Your goal is a collection of conventions that fit together and respond well to most of the situations you encounter at the table.

— — — — — —

The final issue raised in this book is are you really aware of the strengths and weaknesses in your game? If you are, you have a head start on the next and final chapter. Its purpose is to significantly advance your game through a self-study program.

Chapter 10

YOUR OWN SELF-STUDY PROGRAM

This chapter offers a program for your further development as a bridge player. Everyone has differing strengths and weaknesses and therefore different needs. Each one of you who wants to advance should develop a self-study program carefully tailored to your own needs. Any areas of your game which are troublesome to you or which produce poor results at the table should be prime candidates for a self-study program. In developing your program, use the literature and computer programs discussed below as well as related material in other chapters on the best thinking of experts. In addition, for those of you who wish to advance even further, study carefully the tendencies and traits of world class players at the end of this chapter.

THE CURRENT AND RELEVANT LITERATURE

Over the past 75 years many hundreds of books have been written on bridge. Our criteria for including a particular book in the literature are stringent. The book must be:

- Substantive
- Contemporary or a *still relevant* classic
- Easy to read and understand

In other words, at best you will learn a lot from the books listed below and at worst none of them will be a disappointment to you.

Bidding

On the subject of *bidding* the dominant force today is Mike Lawrence. His books cover practically every facet of bidding. They are thorough, use an easy style of presentation and are very well written. In discussing bidding issues with you, he is ever mindful that, first and foremost, bridge is a partnership game. Books by Marty Bergen and Larry Cohen also have had a major influence on modern thinking.

Best Available Literature - Bidding

- Better Bidding with Bergen (Volumes 1 & 2)   Bergen
- Points Schmoints   Bergen
- To Bid or Not to Bid - The Law of Total Tricks   Cohen

- Two-Over-One Game Force   Hardy
- Practical Slam Bidding   Klinger
- Contested Auctions   Lawrence
- The Complete Book on   Lawrence
    Hand Evaluation
    Overcalls
    Balancing
    Takeout Doubles

- Passed Hand Bidding   Lawrence

- Topics on Bridge - Series #1   Lawrence
    (Reverses, Overcalls, Responding to an Overcall,
    Bidding Versus an Opening One Notrump,
    Bidding After an Opponent's Takeout Double,
    Responding to a Takeout Double,
    Bidding Over Preempts, Weak Two Bids,
    The Fine Art of Hanging Partner, The Splinter Bid)

- Topics on Bridge - Series #2   Lawrence
    (When Should You Make a Penalty Double - Parts
    1 & 2, Mistakes You Should Stop Making - Parts
    1 & 2, When Can You Overcall With a Four-Card
    Suit?, How Long is Partner's Suit?, Preempts,
    The Takeout Double, Balancing)

- D.O.N.T. (Disturbing Opponents NoTrump)   Lawrence
- Stronger Competitive Bidding   Miles

- Commonsense Bidding   Root

Figure 10-1

Because of the importance of *competitive bidding* in any form of bridge, books dealing with that subject should receive your attention. If your preference is for short treatments of special bidding issues, we again refer you to Mike Lawrence who has published many excellent topical pamphlets.

Declarer Play

On the subject of *declarer play* there are a number of very fine classics, including a timeless one, Card Play Technique, by Mollo and Gardener. The most prolific writer in this area is Kelsey. His books are so clearly written that he can easily communicate to the average player even the most complex declarer play problems. Kantar and Reese also have done excellent work in this field. Their books contain challenging problem hands whose solutions are based on wide-ranging principles. Further, their books make lively and interesting reading.

Best Available Literature - Declarer Play

• Dormer on Deduction	Dormer
• Bridge with the Blue Team	Forquet
• A New Approach to Play and Defense (Volumes 1 & 2)	Kantar
• Take Your Tricks	Kantar
• Creative Card Play	Kauder
• Countdown to Better Bridge	Kelsey
• The Tough Game	Kelsey
• Challenge Match	Kelsey
• Strip Squeezes	Kelsey
• Card Combinations	Lawrence
• Play Bridge With Mike Lawrence	Lawrence
• Topics on Bridge - Series #2 (Endplays, The Simple Squeeze, The Loser on Loser Play, Timing)	Lawrence
• All 52 Cards	Miles
• Card Play Technique	Mollo & Gardener
• Reese on Play	Reese
• Master Play	Reese
• Play Bridge With Reese	Reese
• That Elusive Extra Trick	Reese & Bird
• The Extra Edge in Play	Reese/Pottage
• How to Play a Bridge Hand	Root

Figure 10-2

The **declarer play** books in Figure 10-2, are instructive and fun to read. Some even do a great job of recreating the atmosphere at the table during a tournament. The result is you feel as if you are actually there playing the hand in a tournament environment.

Defense

For several decades no one seriously ventured into the most difficult part of bridge - **defense** - in any comprehensive way. Among the first to enter the field were Kelsey's early classic, <u>Killing Defense</u>, and Kantar's instructive problem-solving books. Then, during the 1980s several books emerged which began to attack the whole subject of defense on broader, more comprehensive lines. The first of these was <u>Winning Defense for an Advancing Bridge Player</u> by Stewart. Other books have followed, including ones by Root and the Granovetters.

Best Available Literature - Defense

• A Switch in Time	Granovetters
• Complete Defensive Bridge Play	Kantar
• Kantar for the Defense	Kantar
• A New Approach to Play and Defense (Volumes 1 & 2)	Kantar
• Defensive Tips for Bad Card Holders	Kantar
• Killing Defense	Kelsey
• Test Your Defensive Play	Kelsey
• Dynamic Defense	Lawrence
• Topics on Bridge - Series #1 (Defense - Part 1, Defense - Part 2, Signals on Defense)	Lawrence
• Topics on Bridge - Series #2 (Third Hand Play, Suit Preference)	Lawrence
• Defensive Signals	Miles
• How to Defend a Bridge Hand	Root
• Winning Defense for an Advancing Bridge Player	Stewart
• The Bridge Player's Comprehensive Guide to Defense	Stewart
• Partnership Defense	Woolsey

Figure 10-3

Opening Leads

Because of the importance of **opening leads** to successful defense, books on that subject are in considerable demand. An early classic by Ewen stood alone for a long time. Then, Blackwood covered the subject in the 1980s and finally a new one by Lawrence in 1996. In the new book by Lawrence, you can find most everything you've wanted to know about opening leads, and more. Much of the book is devoted to diagnosing revealing auctions as a means of finding the right lead - if there is one. An additional bonus in the book are insights on the bidding process itself.

Best Available Literature - Opening Leads

• Complete Book of Opening Leads	Blackwood
• Opening Leads	Ewen
• 50 Winning Duplicate Tips	Klinger
• Opening Leads	Lawrence
• Topics on Bridge - Series #1 (Leads Versus Notrump, Leads Versus Suit Contracts)	Lawrence

Figure 10-4

Team Tactics

Not much has been written on **team tactics**. The one book to date on theory is Winning Swiss Team Tactics by Feldheim. Perhaps the quickest way to get a handle on the unique aspects of team events is to review the ACBL Pamphlet on the subject and from time to time scan our Chapter 7 highlights (figures 7-1 to 7-4). Some challenging and interesting practice sessions are available in three other books listed in Figure 10-5, two by Kelsey and one by Lawrence.

Best Available Literature - Team Tactics

• ACBL Pamphlet, Swiss Team Tactics	ACBL
• Winning Swiss Team Tactics	Feldheim
• The Tough Game	Kelsey
• Challenge Match	Kelsey
• Playing a Swiss Team of Four	Lawrence

Figure 10-5

Matchpoint Strategy and Conventions

Although limited discussion of **matchpoint strategy and conventions** are embodied in many books, few have devoted themselves exclusively to these subjects. Perhaps the all-time best on matchpoint strategy and tactics is the Kelsey classic, Matchpoint Bridge. Over the years the best book on conventions has been the one by Root and Pavlicek. It explains many of the conventions that have been in regular use and includes detailed illustrations of how they work.

Best Available Literature - Matchpoint Strategy and Conventions

• Everyone's Guide to the New Convention Card	Bergen
• Conventions At a Glance	Granovetter
• Bridge Conventions Complete	Kearse
• Matchpoint Bridge	Kelsey
• 50 Winning Duplicate Tips	Klinger
• Modern Bridge Conventions	Root & Pavlicek
• Matchpoints	Woolsey

Figure 10-6

Entertainment

In the field of **entertainment** the number one best seller of all times is the hilarious book Why You Lose at Bridge by Simon. It has endured the test of time, entertaining players for almost half a century. If you want some fascinating reading on the lives of world class players at the bridge table, try those by Zia Mahmood and Bob Hamman. And, if you want to read a book that is hard to put down try How to Play Bridge With Your Spouse (and Survive). This one is extremely well written, informative and is fun to read for **all** types of partnerships.

Best Available Literature - Entertainment

• Right Through the Pack	Darvas & Hart
• At the Table, My Life and Times	Hamman
• Play Bridge With Mike Lawrence	Lawrence
• Bridge My Way	Zia Mahmood
• Bridge in the Menagerie	Mollo
• Bridge Exploits of the Monks of St. Titus	Reese & Bird
• Why You Lose at Bridge	Simon
• How to Play Bridge With Your Spouse (and Survive)	Teukolsky

Figure 10-7

PLAYING BRIDGE AGAINST THE COMPUTER

Playing bridge against the computer is an excellent way to work on various aspects of your game. You may work on play of the hand (different skill levels are available), bid hands with the latest conventions or practice defending. Some computer programs also generate hands to your own particular specifications so that you can practice bidding with your regular partners. In this way you can experiment with new conventions or practice hands that are causing you difficulty at the table.

251

The best available computer programs listed in Figure 10-8 are just a snapshot in time. Although not able to seriously challenge experts, such programs are continuously making advances and their potential seems unlimited. The listing is based upon analysis done by the ACBL, considering user friendliness, bridge logic, graphics quality and customer service.

Best Available Computer Programs

- GIB
- Bridge Baron 9.01.02
- Q-plus Bridge v.5.5
- Micro Bridge 8.06
- Bridge Buff 7.0
- Saitek Pro Bridge 510
- Endless Bridge 4.1

- Meadowlark Bridge 1.36
- Blue Chip Bridge 3.0.0
- Bicycle Bridge
- Oxford Bridge 5.1
- Bridge Master Class II
- Bridge Deluxe II
- Bridge Mate 3

Figure 10-8

Each of the listed computer programs perform all bridge functions and have particular features which make them individually attractive. These features include fast and friendly, excellent graphics, lots of conventions and the ability to play hands from actual tournaments. Some feature bridge duplicate matches scored by the computer or against deals played in ACBL tournaments.

A NEW FUN WAY TO LEARN

A new teaching tool has emerged in the form of interactive CDs. A number of excellent ones are already on the market. They include ones on defense and counting by Mike Lawrence and on events from national tournaments by Larry Cohen. Here, the bridge player visually goes through actual deals played at major tournaments and either observes or participates in hundreds of key decisions. Then Cohen explains, simply and with humor, how experts make these decisions at the table. This is a fun way of playing in a national tournament with little expense.

ENTERING THE WORLD OF INTERNET BRIDGE

The power and convenience of bridge on the Internet is now a reality. There are various networks which offer the chance for you to play bridge with other people across the country or worldwide. Most networks offer a free trial to see if you would like to subscribe to their service.

Network Bridge Services

- Bridge Player Live
- EBU Online Bridge Club
- Floater
- Microsoft Network Gaming Zone
- OKbridge
- Pogo.com
- WinBridge
- Yahoo Games

Figure 10-9

These networks provide outstanding graphics and the chance to play some really good bridge with people at your level anywhere in the world. New friends or partnerships can be formed through these experiences. In addition, experts located in different parts of the country practice for major events over these networks. Periodically, they put on exhibitions for spectators.

OK Bridge is a 24-hour duplicate bridge club open to people around the world. OK Bridge became the first network to conduct on-line duplicate tournaments, including matchpoints, IMPs and teams. It has more than 17000 members from over 90 countries.

The play in network bridge can take place within a variety of rooms to suit different types and standards of play, including duplicate play and rubber bridge. The ACBL awards limited master points in duplicate events conducted on the Internet. You can link up to any of these Internet services on ACBL's home page at www.acbl.org. On the same home page players can keep up with tournament results and many other activities going on in the bridge world.

SOME FINAL THOUGHTS ON HOW TO ADVANCE YOUR BRIDGE PLAY

Aside from following the expert roadmap in this book, there are several things you can work on to advance your bridge game even further. These are the special tendencies and traits which have enabled experts to be consistently successful in national and international competitions, thereby transforming themselves into *World Class players*.

Tendencies/Traits of World Class Players

• Consistently play in tough competition
• Stamina
• The "X Factor"
• Temperament
• Discipline
• Concentration
• Table presence

Figure 10-10

Consistently Play in Tough Competition

The best way of all to accelerate your development as a bridge player is to consistently play in tough competition. This is something you have to decide for yourself. It means curtailing your short-term interest in winning master points in easier events in favor of becoming the very best you can be. For example, if you are a Flight B player, play in Flight A events. If you are a senior, play in open events. If you are a Flight A player, play in National rather than Regional events at the North American Bridge Championships (NABC). And, while you are at national tournaments, take a couple of days off to kibitz some of the world class players - it's fun and informative.

Eventually, the master points will catch up to you - and much faster than you may think.

Stamina

To withstand the stress of day in and day out top-level competition requires stamina and plenty of it. This is easy to say - difficult to develop.

To illustrate the importance of stamina, some top players have gone into physical training several months before a world championship. Developing stamina goes hand-in-hand with consistently playing in top competition. It is difficult to achieve one without the other. Obviously, avoiding big meals and alcohol between sessions is helpful.

The "X Factor"

The "X factor" was described in an ACBL bulletin article* as an elusive quality that transcends talent - guts, competitive spirit, killer instinct. People with the "X factor" never give up. They summon all their resources and go for the throat (jugular) until the bitter end. The classic situation in bridge is when the opponents are in an iron clad contract and a defender, refusing to give up, finds a way (such as a trump uppercut) to defeat the contract. All top players have the "X factor."

Temperament

To do well in top-level competition you must develop the temperament to "roll with the punches," shake off the many ups and downs and *go on to the next hand*. This was the theme in an excellent book about life at the table of a world champion.

> **"No amount of recrimination, self-flagellation or excuse making can change the result. Indulging in such exercises does nothing but distract you from the task at hand - which is the next board you're supposed to play."**
> **- Bob Hamman**

---

* "The X Factor," Roselyn Teukolsky, ACBL Bulletin, January 1996.

Another expert quoted from the famous author, Rudyard Kipling to make a similar point.

> "... the deadliest assaults on your concentra -tion come from within ... whether it be anger at your partner's sloppy defense ... or elation (over a good result) ... the player must learn, as Kipling puts it, 'to meet with triumph and disaster and treat those two imposters just the same'."
> — Hugh Kelsey

Discipline

There are times at the table when you know (or think you know) what is the right thing to do but somehow cannot bring yourself to do it. Making it happen - that is, doing the **right thing** time after time, regardless of the pressures - is a matter of discipline. Some illustrations of discipline are:

- Resisting the temptation, in competition, to raise the level of bidding beyond the law of total tricks
- Making a very difficult opening lead when the bidding suggests that it is the right thing to do
- Postponing the drawing of trumps until a side suit is established
- Staying with the field in matchpoints.

Top players have developed the discipline to do the **right thing** time after time under pressure. They do so because they know from experience that over the long term it pays off.

Concentration

Within the expert community, concentration is perhaps the most widely talked about mark of a champion. In fact, mistakes at the higher levels of bridge are almost always caused by a lapse of concentration. Experts know they must stay focused on the immediate hand if they expect to play or defend it properly. You can do the same if you train yourself to ignore distractions of all kinds. Further, most experts believe that **partnership** has a great influence on your degree of concentration. One put it this way:

> **"If partner makes you feel good about your-self, you feel comfortable. Comfort is the key to relaxation. Relaxation is the key to concentration, and concentration is the key to maximum performance."**
> **-Zeke Jabbour**

Table Presence

Finally, there is the all-important matter called "table presence." People with table presence literally work out in some magical way what's going on at the table. They use inferences, deductive reasoning, and, like any good poker player, they learn to read their opponents.

> **"We must constantly ask ourselves why the other players have done *or* not done what they might have done."**
> **- Albert Dormer**

Experts who acquire table presence concentrate on what's going on, ask themselves the right questions, and use logic or deductive reasoning to figure out the hand *and* their opponents! This includes making a judgment as to their opponents' level of skill and any subtle clues about their hand. At the same time, experts train themselves not to give away information about their own holdings so that their opponents will not succeed in reading them.

A questioning and problem-solving mind is essential to developing keen table presence. Anyone who has a flair for the game and who loves deductive reasoning and problem solving has a great chance of reaching celebrity status in the bridge world.

- - - - - -

As you proceed on your quest to become a better player or even to join the ranks of the experts, you will find that improvement comes gradually and may not even be noticeable to you! However, it will be noticable to your partners and to your opponents.

We wish you the very best and, remember, it really is within your grasp to become a much better player.

Appendix

MATCHPOINT SCORING

In a matchpoint event, your competitors are the players who hold your cards the other times that same deal is played. You receive one point for each pair you beat and one-half point for each pair you tie. How much you outscore them by is unimportant. Just ten points is enough.

Take the case of a typical partscore contract below (both sides vulnerable).

Partscore Contract

Contract	Result	N/S Score	Matchpoints
2♠	Made 2	110	7½
2♠	Made 2	110	7½
2♠	Made 2	110	7½
2♠	Made 2	110	7½
2♠	Made 2	110	7½
2♠	Made 2	110	7½
2♠	Made 3	140	11
1NT	Made 1	90	2
3♦(DBL)	Down 1	200	12
3♦	Down 1	100	3½
3♦	Down 1	100	3½
3♠	Down 1	-100	½
3♠	Down 1	-100	½

Notice that about half of the field played two of a major suit. Only one of the N/S pairs made an extra trick but in matchpoints that extra 30 points gave them a near top board. The next pair got into an inferior contract and scored 90 - a very poor result - although the difference in score was nominal.

The next N/S pair, rather than take a push to the three level, decided to double their opponents. Their reward was a top board because their opponents were vulnerable, down one - the **Magic 200**. The next two pairs also refused to take the push to the 3 level, but they let the opponents play their contract undoubled, and got a poor score. The final two N/S pairs made the mistake of taking the push to the three level and their result (down one) got them a bottom board.

A typical game contract in a matchpoint event follows, with neither side vulnerable.

Game Contract

Contract	Result	N/S Score	Matchpoints
2♥	Made 4	170	3½
3♥	Made 4	170	3½
4♥	Made 4	420	8½
4♥	Made 4	420	8½
4♥	Made 4	420	8½
4♥	Made 4	420	8½
4♥	Made 5	450	11
3NT	Made 3	400	6
5♣(DBL)	Down 2	300	5
5♣(DBL)	Down 3	500	12
5♥	Down 1	-50	1½
5♥	Down 1	-50	1½
5♥(DBL)	Down 1	-100	0

The first two N/S pairs missed an obvious game and paid the price. Five others reached game and one managed an overtrick, giving that pair a near top board. The next pair got to the wrong contract and received a below average score. The E/W opponents of the last five pairs got into the action and took a sacrifice, rather than let the N/S pairs play at the game level. The first of these five N/S pairs doubled but only defeated the contract by two tricks; plus 300 was below average for them. The next pair doubled, defended very well and earned a top score for their efforts. The last three N/S pairs took the push to the five level, went down, and got very poor matchpoint scores.

As any one who plays matchpoints knows, there are variables at times over which you have absolutely no control. For example, there is luck involved in who you play certain hands against; that is, luck is with you if you play your more difficult hands against less skilled opponents. Also, there are the "fixes," such as a strange bid or lead that produces an unreasonably poor result. This kind of thing happens to everyone.

HOW TO ORDER ADDITIONAL COPIES

To treat a friend to a copy of this book or to order additional copies please add $3.00 postage and handling to the list price, and send check or money order to: Burt and Lynn Hall, 6260 Grand Cypress Circle, Lake Worth, Florida, 33463.